Cohousing

in Britain

Edited by

Sarah Bunker

Chris Coates

Martin Field

Jonathan How

A Diggers & Dreamers Review

DIGGERS AND DREAMERS PUBLICATIONS

Diggers & Dreamers
Publications
2011

First published
2011
D&D Publications
BCM Edge
London
WC1N 3XX

ISBN
978-0-9545757-3-1
Paperback

Front cover illustration
Sarah Bunker

Back cover photographs (clockwise from top left):
- LILAC (© white design)
- Threshold (Threshold Community)
- Forgebank
- Springhill (Martin Field)

Distribution
Edge of Time Ltd
BCM Edge
London
WC1N 3XX
www.edgeoftime.co.uk

Typesetting and Layout
Sarah Bunker
Jonathan How

Acknowledgements: Thank you to all our contributors and especially to Martin Field (author of *Thinking about Cohousing*), who is our guest editor for this first Diggers & Dreamers Review; his expertise, professionalism and patience have been much appreciated. Once again we've been to several places for our meetings in the last two years, so grateful thanks to everyone at Springhill, Postlip Hall, Monkton Wyld, and the Field and Coates homes in Leicester for being such generous hosts. We remain indebted to Belinda Whitworth for her excellent proof-reading – any errors that remain are ours!

Contents

Preface

ANGELA BRADY

74th President of the Royal Institute of British Architects.

The time for cohousing is now. If you want to live within a caring community and grow together with friends as neighbours, be valued as part of a large 'family group' and live sustainably - then this housing lifestyle is for you.

I first came across cohousing in 1981 when I won a post graduate scholarship to study community housing in Denmark. I spent 18 months travelling between all 34 'Boffaelleskaber' projects that existed at that time. Today, 50,000 people live in cohousing projects in Denmark (1% of the population), and its popularity is spreading. This 'new form' of community housing seemed to me to be so ideal, so utopian and perfect for sociable people who want to know their neighbours and share everyday chores like cooking and child minding in order to make time for important things in life like family and friends or developing a shared hobby like art, music or drama.

It was by chance that I came across the architect Jan Gudman Huyer who had started the Danish cohousing movement 10 years earlier with a cohousing group of 33 homes at Skraplanet where they lived. I returned a couple of years ago with a film crew and met Jan and his wife 28 years later - still there with the second generation of their community starting similar cohousing projects and continuing the same lifestyle.

I have spoken about this ideal way of living for decades without getting much of a response in the UK, so I am particularly delighted that cohousing is proving itself and is gaining momentum. I look forward to visiting LILAC and other new projects underway. If ever the time was right to build community housing it is now, with government policy promoting a community right to build and community-led sustainable building proposals. I hope to see cohousing blossom.

At the RIBA, as part of our September 2011 'Homewise' campaign, we set up a housing commission to look into how we live today and what our current needs are. I believe that there is a strong need for alternative ways of living, like cohousing, where people who value caring and sharing can create their own ideal way of living for the next 50 years and beyond.

Introduction: How Far Has Cohousing in the UK Come?

MARTIN FIELD

Our Diggers & Dreamers guest editor maps the terrain of cohousing in the UK.

This new publication from the Diggers & Dreamers collective is focused upon a look at how cohousing is faring in the UK and is a follow-up to the previous release of *Thinking about Cohousing* in 2004. It is being issued at a time when there is a very keen upsurge of interest in all kinds of mutual and collaborative approaches to meeting housing and community needs, including interest at the highest political levels for how communities can take more control over their housing and neighbourhood ideals.

The fragilities and catastrophes of recent events in the property and finance markets have brought many concerns forward about how non-egalitarian and divisive the UK has become in its mainstream approaches to meeting social concerns. Largely through the long-standing persistence of the broad co-operative movement, a report promoting the alternatives from mutual housing opportunities was drawn up in 2009 for the Labour Government by the Commission on Co-operative and Mutual Housing[1], which concluded how 'many housing organisations now recognise the value of community, [and] are taking steps towards co-operation and mutuality ...', alongside identifying steps that sympathetic organisations could take to support mutuality in practice. The UK Cohousing Network was a core member of the Commission, and the concept of cohousing features significantly in the final text. An egalitarian sharing of decision-making and the long-term benefits of new neighbourhood provisions remains at the core of cohousing proposals, and they rightly can be assessed alongside other mutual formats for such strength and benefits. On the back of that report, a body of representatives from across the mutual sector has since emerged (representing housing co-ops, land trusts, tenant management bodies, local authority housing management organisations, cohousing groups and others) that is already achieving significant success in lobbying for new funds and development opportunities that could be targeted towards a variety of new mutual housing developments – whether this be co-ops, cohousing schemes, community land trusts, or others.

Such mutual values are clearly supported by the Coalition Government's present 'localism' agenda. This has been heralded as a complete shake-up of local services and local bureaucracies and, ultimately, to be a means whereby changes to the built environment would be at the behest of local communities, rather than over their heads. Current proposals for new legislation have therefore included a number of innovative mechanisms to stimulate community engagement in the dynamics of neighbourhood planning and development. These include the much-reported 'community right to build' and the identification of local assets for community-focused purposes. There are also other high-level working groups examining how all aspects of self-build/community-build developments could be promoted in the future.

It is interesting to see how directly the government has promoted its intention to receive ideas for its 'right to build' opportunity, including a web-page flyer (see right) on how local people might progress co-ops, or cohousing, or other kinds of community-led developments (!), and a new report on how to support communities commissioning all kinds of self-build projects[2].

What can be said about the current 'localism' debate is that it is certainly attempting to articulate a straightforward ambition: it poses questions about how to stimulate community engagement with the planning of local services, and how to gain community 'buy-in' for changes that could be proposed to the character of local places. The political rhetoric that has been flying back and forth to date has, however, been largely focused on contrasting views as to whether or not this 'localism' will result in significant quantities of new house-building to help the nation's perceived shortage in supply, or whether it will just promote a rise in NIMBYism (and it does have some potential

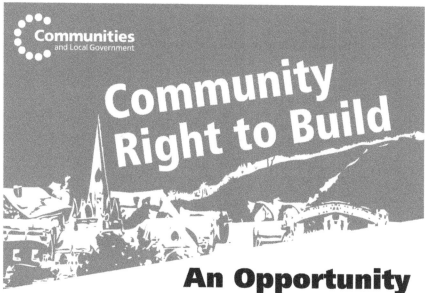

An Opportunity in the Making

The Government is planning to give citizens more rights to decide what is built in their communities, including housing, local shops and community facilities.

Proposals for the Community Right to Build are currently before Parliament as part of the neighbourhood planning framework in the Localism Bill. If the Bill becomes law any successful proposal will need to be:

- from a community group such as a community interest company or a community land trust, etc

- independently assessed to see whether the proposals meet specific key criteria; and

- supported by more than half of the community that vote in a referendum.

If you're interested in a community-led development you should talk to your neighbours to get an idea about what sort of development the whole community would want to see. You may also want to talk to your local council, housing association or other community groups. You may also find it useful to get advice from people who already have experience of taking forward community-led schemes.

To find out more about the Community Right to Build visit:
www.communities.gov.uk/righttobuild
for further information.

If your community group is interested in using the Community Right to Build and wants to be kept in touch, tell us about your plans at:

righttobuild@communities.gsi.gov.uk

For information on community led developments, visit:

Community Land Trust Network –
www.communitylandtrusts.org.uk

Locality –
www.locality.org.uk

UK Cohousing Network –
www.cohousing.org.uk

Action with Communities in Rural England –
www.acre.org.uk/our-work/community-led-planning

Confederation of Co-operative Housing –
www.cch.coop

for either ...). It has been less overtly engaged with what particular qualities will be central to such new developments, and less vocal about how to craft new neighbourhoods, as distinct from the numbers of new housing units or other new 'community facilities'.

It is significant, therefore, that an interest in creating new neighbourhoods remains persistent in the UK – certainly if judged by the widespread nature of cohousing groups on the ground and their plans for building new neighbourhoods. The UK Cohousing Network has a constant stream of contacts seeking information and advice, and regular requests are received from media sources interested in writing new magazine pieces, or in making small documentaries about the modern-day cohousing experience. There is a steady focus upon cohousing and other mutual housing philosophies from the academic sector, producing papers and dissertational pieces that relate cohousing's key characteristics to the British community scene, and making contributions to international meetings, like last year's comprehensive conference in Sweden. The option of cohousing provision as a choice for older people is being discussed and debated more and more by policy-makers, and specifically as an alternative to traditionally minded sheltered-housing or extra-care schemes[3]. Government departments have noted "a growing interest among older people in cohousing communities where they can control their own self-contained accommodation and live as a mutually supportive group with some common space". Cohousing has also now broken the barrier of being recognised in central mechanisms to provide public housing grants towards the costs of appropriate new development, and the first grant-assisted project has already been completed in Dorset.

Yet, putting such activities and engagements to one side, the actual creation of new cohousing neighbourhoods in the UK over the past few years remains very modest. The most identifiable successes have been Springhill in Stroud – completed during the time that *Thinking about Cohousing* was produced – and the development and occupation of the UK's first cross-tenure cohousing project at the Threshold Centre in Dorset. In the wings, there are the high-spec 'eco-projects' about to commence work on-site at Forgebank in Halton, Lancaster, and the LILAC project in Leeds, now also with full planning permission and looking to be on-site this year. Other groups have remained persistent and focused for quite some considerable time – such as the OWCH group in London, or the development plans in Brighton – but it would not be honest to talk up the number of new UK cohousing neighbourhoods that people have been able to create.

There also continue to be other UK projects that commentators describe as representing cohousing developments – small neighbourhood housing projects that plan a shared use of facilities or land, or groupings of new houses that intend to maximise interactions between neighbours. The UK Network continues to hear of ideas to include 'three or four cohousing properties' within plans for a wider housing development, though by the nature of this scale they would not be able to create the cohousing dynamic in practice. At one level this is an encouraging sign of support for aspects of communal living within wider development plans, although at another it sounds like a confusion remains on what is identifiably unique to making cohousing neighbourhoods the viable communities they are. It is worth repeating that the core characteristics of cohousing neighbourhoods[4] are:

(a) Designing in order to create intentional neighbourhoods.

(b) A minimum provision of essential private and common facilities.

(c) A size and scale suitable to foster and sustain the necessary community dynamics.

(d) Cohousing residents having the final say about all aspects of their neighbourhood.

[See Appendix A for further details]

So, whilst this is not to be disparaging about all kinds of housing development that can help support sustainable communities, claims that very disparate approaches are, or will be, cohousing approaches can still point to a lack of clarity as to just what distinguishes the cohousing approach from that of other kinds of housing or mutual development. It needs to be clearly emphasised that the cohousing philosophy is very focused upon creating neighbourhoods – its promotion of collective responsibilities is not solely based upon a collaborative approach to the building of houses, or the management of new homes. It is what the cohousing movement in the United States has memorably summarised as 'creating communities, one neighbourhood at a time ...'. It is a philosophy that encompasses a focus on the quality of house-building and the physical setting for homes, within an embracive attention given to a whole set of interpersonal and shared community dynamics.

It might be hoped that the distinctive qualities which cohousing schemes routinely achieve – outcomes that are certainly not customarily found within mainstream UK housing provision – could be sufficient grounds for such schemes to be utilised more widely in UK building projects. If this is not yet happening because of a lack of practical information for fitting cohousing into the UK's context of contemporary concerns – such as how it can square with demands to help provide 'affordable' housing – then the chapters that follow should provide plenty to consider. Perspectives and information are provided on both historic and up-to-date considerations about the cohousing momentum in the UK, alongside observations about how the cohousing approach sits within the wider context of British housing, neighbourhood and mutual develop-ments as a whole.

Finally a 'cohousing-centric' vision for the future is suggested, in order to set a challenge for making the process of creating this distinctive kind of neighbour-hood just a little bit more straight-forward ... it would be good if building new communities didn't exhaust people and so prevent them from enjoying the results!

Notes
1. *Bringing Democracy Home*, Commission on Co-operative & Mutual Housing (2009)

2. *An Action Plan to promote the growth of self-build housing in the UK*, DCLG and National Self-build Association (2011)

3. *Lifetime Homes, Lifetime Neighbourhoods: a National Strategy for Housing in an Ageing Society*, DCLG/Dept of Health Publications (2008)

4. Abridged text taken from *Thinking about Cohousing*, M. Field, Diggers & Dreamers Publications (2004)

Martin Field
works at the Institute for Urban Affairs at the University of Northampton

From Co-housekeeping to Cohousing

CHRIS COATES

Did genteel co-operation 150 years ago set a UK precedent for cohousing?

> *... a system for improving the quality of home life, in which several households of one or more people combined to share the costs and labour involved in providing themselves with services such as cooking, laundry and cleaning. Households retained their individual homes and privacy, but ate some meals in a communal dining room and shared other communal facilities. Ideally, co-operative homes would be situated close together, and centred on a specially built complex of buildings containing the dining room, central kitchen and common room.*
> Lynn F. Pearson – The Architectural and Social History of Co-operative Living

The above passage describes not some Danish or American cohousing scheme from the last quarter of the 20th century, but rather a housing model with its roots in a Victorian movement known as co-operative housekeeping. With links to both the co-operative and the early feminist movements, and later with those involved in the Garden Cities, co-operative housekeeping provided a model for shared housing that lasted up to and beyond the Second World War. As far back as 1850 in an article titled 'Associated Homes for Poor Ladies' in *The Leader* Oct 1850, the political writer Harriet Martineau had advocated the formation of Associated Homes of 20 'Ladies' living together in a large house. Each woman would have her own rooms and share sitting room, library and communal meals together as an alternative to cheap lodgings for single women living in the city. Both *The Co-Operator* and *Co-operative News* carried a number of articles on domestic co-operation in the 1860s and 70s. Several

Homesgarth: in the quadrangle[1]

articles appeared giving details of an American experiment, the Cambridge Co-operative Housekeeping Society, which had been started by a Mrs Melusina Pierce in 1869. Using the British Co-operative Movement as an example, she had devised a scheme for applying co-operative principles to the domestic economy. In a series of articles in the *Atlantic Monthly* Mrs Pierce put forward the suggestions for a group of 12 to 50 families living in small blocks of houses surrounded by gardens sited around a co-operative housekeeping centre where the women would share the household tasks as part of a sort of housekeeping co-op. Charges would be made for the services and any profits from the scheme would be returned to investors. The 'housekeeping centre' would include kitchen, laundry, sewing room and gymnasium. Meals would be delivered to individual homes by horse and cart. Mrs Pierce's main aim was to find a role for increasingly marginalised middle-class women, and although she envisaged women-only meetings to organise the work, she made the mistake of making the highest decision-making authority a council of all the male heads of household who unanimously dissolved the Society in 1871.

The *Atlantic Monthly* was widely read in middle-class homes in England and Mrs Pierce's ideas were given a warm if somewhat muted reception in the pages of other housekeeping magazines of the time. The idea of co-operative housekeeping was taken up by Mrs Elizabeth Moss King, a prolific writer and speaker, member of the British Association for the Advancement of Science and founding secretary of the Rational Dress Society. She managed to get wide publicity for her ideas – *The Times* reported on a paper given to the annual meeting of the British Association entitled 'Confederated Homes & Co-operative Housekeeping', stating that Mrs King's paper was the chief attraction of the day. *The Englishwoman's Review* and *The Queen* also carried reports on the lecture and the president of the meeting suggested at the end that the time had come for a practical experiment in co-operative house-keeping to be set up. Through Mrs King's advocacy the idea of shared forms of housekeeping circulated widely among middle-class circles, being picked up by those women becoming involved in the growing women's suffrage movement. Mrs King went as far as to commission plans for a co-operative home from the architect Edward W Godwin which were printed in the April 1874 edition of *Building News*. They showed a block of flats for over 100 adults with a communal dining room, kitchen and play facilities for children. Designed to look as uninstitutional as possible it was 'neither a huge barrack – nor a flaunting hotel'.

Edward Vansittart Neale, a leading figure in the Co-operative Movement, had become an advocate of associated homes in the 1860s and in 1872 he detailed plans for a series of five-storey blocks of flats with a separate building for various communal facilities. The article in *Co-operative News* in January 1872 listed the communal facilities as including a central kitchen and dining room, laundry, bathrooms, library, smoking and billiard rooms and a nursery, with the suggestion that school rooms and gardens could be added if desired by the residents. The response to proposals for model homes in blocks of flats was generally lukewarm. They smacked of tenement provision for the poor and were seen as a middle-class idea being foisted onto the working class when working class aspirations were for small individual houses. A competition in the August 1887 issue of the monthly *Work and Leisure* magazine, to design a block of associated dwellings for single women earning between 20 shillings and 90 shillings a week, brought two poor responses from its readers. Undeterred, the editor published her own proposals unremarkable in themselves were it not for the fact that the editor, Louisa M. Hubbard, followed up her sug-gestions by setting up the Ladies' Dwelling Company to make the plan a reality. After over 40 years of talk about associated homes and co-operative housekeep-ing there was 'suddenly' a flurry of activity. Another company, Ladies' Residential Chambers Ltd., was registered and construction work started on two blocks of women's flats. The first to open was in Chenies St, Bloomsbury, built by Ladies' Residential Chambers Ltd in May 1889. The opening of the six-storey, unshaped block of self contained flats, complete with common dining room and kitchen, was attended by well-known figures in the women's movement including Lydia Becker, Clementina Black and Elizabeth Garrett Anderson. Three months later Sloane Gardens House was opened by the Ladies' Dwelling Company just off Sloane Square. It catered for 106 women, providing a public restaurant, reception room, music rooms and studios. Single rooms and sets of rooms were for hire, a lady housekeeper was present and there were four shops at street level.

Among those drawn to the idea of co-operative house-keeping were those involved in the embryonic Garden City Movement. Ebenezer Howard himself, founder of the movement and author of *Garden Cities of Tomorrow*, put forward a scheme designed by H. C. Lander in 1906 in an illustrated article in the *Daily Mail*. It was for a leafy tree-strewn quadrangle of co-operative houses, each with its own sitting room, hall, scullery with gas stove, bathroom and from one to three bedrooms. From the common kitchen, dining room and administration block sited on one side of the quadrangle 'shared servants' would service the houses. Howard suggested that this was of benefit to both the householders who would save money and enjoy greater privacy and the servants themselves who would enjoy greater freedom than if they worked for a single household. A company, Letchworth Co-operative Houses, was formed in 1907 to take the project forward: on offer to prospective tenants were private gardens, the use of shared sports facilities and vegetarian meals. The scheme, named 'Homesgarth', as built consisted of accommodation for 16 households on two sides of a quadrangle linked together by a covered walkway with a three-storey accommodation block containing a dining room, seating up to 60 people on the ground floor. Above it (to minimise cooking smells) was the central kitchen and staff accommodation. Built on a site facing Sollershot Circus, leased to the company by First Garden City Ltd for a nominal rent, Homesgarth ran as a co-operative housekeeping scheme for nearly 40 years. Howard and his second wife moved in in 1911 and lived there until 1921. Reaction to the scheme was mixed but generally supportive and in some instances downright enthusiastic. Lucy Carr Shaw, Bernard Shaw's sister, wrote to Howard in 1913 that after being 'nearly worried to death by the cares of housekeeping and the intolerable incompetence of servants ... One of your Co-op houses presents itself to me as a paradise after the turmoil of private housekeeping'. Co-op housekeeping continued at Homesgarth until after WWII, having changed its name to Sollershot Hall in the 1920s.

Others in the Garden City movement were keen to experiment with shared housing. Alice Melvin, secretary of Brent Garden Village, set up The Society for the Promotion of Co-operative Housekeeping and House service. In conjunction with the Co-operative Garden City Committee, whose secretary was H. C. Lander, an ambitious scheme for an entire co-operative Garden City to be built at Ruislip and called Melvin Park was proposed. Nothing came of Melvin Park, but a smaller scheme did come into being in 1912 at Golders Green. Known as Melvin Hall, the 30 flats with communal kitchen and dining room carried on as a co-op housekeeping scheme until 1964 when it was demolished for a new block of flats. The seemingly indefatigable Mrs Melvin went on to set up a third scheme, this time in Priory Road, Hampstead. The Melvin Co-operative Residential Society consisted of five large town houses with about ten tenants in each house. High repair bills and low profits forced the scheme to wind up in 1937.

Homesgarth: the dining room[1]

Alice Melvin's work was covered by the feminist press of the time, *The Freewoman,* carrying a number of features and letters on co-operative housekeeping.

At Hampstead Garden Suburb a scheme for the elderly with shared baths, washhouses and baking ovens, the Orchards, was designed by Parker & Unwin for Hampstead Tenants Ltd Co-partnership and a full blown co-operative housekeeping scheme for single women was built by the Improved Industrial Dwellings Company. Waterlow Court, designed by M. H. Baille Scott was made up of 50 flats arranged

Homesgarth: a private sitting room[1]

around a beautiful cloistered courtyard. Each flat had its own living room, bedroom or bed recess, bathroom and scullery. A central dining hall, common room and kitchen were serviced by a small group of servants. Many of the early residents at the court were feminists or suffragists and a strong communal spirit pervaded the place during the first few years.

Back in Letchworth, Ruth Pym and Miss S. E. Dewe persuaded the Howard Cottage Society to build a co-op housekeeping scheme on Meadow Way Green. In all, nine cottages and a single flat were built around a communal garden with a (small) central dining room and kitchen. Housekeeping was truly co-operative with tenants taking it in fortnightly turns to be the tenant housekeeper with the only servant being a hired cook. Meadow Way Green was popular and successful, continuing until after WWII as a co-operative housekeeping venture.

Two final co-operative housekeeping schemes were built in the 1920's. St George's Court, which had 32 serviced flats with communal facilities for single women, at Bournville in 1924, and Guessens Court at the second Garden City at Welwyn. Designed by H. C. Lander as a full-blown co-operative housekeeping scheme, Guessens Court was to have been a mix of 20 detached and semi-detached houses surrounding a central block of 40 flats and a three-storey communal servicesblock with restaurant, kitchen and guest rooms. The central services were to be managed co-operatively by the residents. After much delay a revised scheme was opened in 1925 consisting of the communal block and the flats. Tenants were required to spend a minimum sum in the restaurant each week, (encouraged by discount coupons), maids could be hired at hourly rates along with boot cleaning and coal-carrying services. Rents covered use of shared tennis courts and maintenance of the gardens and grounds. During the first five years the restaurant turned a small profit and the scheme as a whole just about paid its way.

Co-operative housekeeping schemes contained all the elements currently being proposed for cohousing projects: a combination of private and communal space, shared meals, shared garden and open space, a 'common house' with various communal facilities. The provision of shared servants seems odd to us now, but domestic help for the middle classes did not fade out until after the Second World War. It was also the forced communality of wartime that tainted communal schemes for a whole generation and that helped to hasten the decline of co-operative housekeeping. The people who were drawn to share domestic arrangements and experiment with co-operative forms of living in the early years of the 20th century were largely those in 'non-standard' households: single women, families in new towns who did not have access to an extended family network, plus those with limited resources who saw co-operative housekeeping as a way of attaining a standard of living that they otherwise would not have been able to afford.

After the war there were other attempts to set up housing schemes that could be seen as an extension of the co-operative housekeeping idea. The most extensive communal proposals for post-war reconstruction were put forward by Sir Charles Reilly who had been Professor of Architecture at the University of Liverpool from 1904 until 1933. Reilly's ideas for what became known as 'Reilly Greens' were developed during a period he spent working on the post-war redevelopment of Birkenhead.

I suggested to the borough engineer that we should make a new layout plan together ... They were pleased with the idea and, chiefly wanting to get a semi-new planning principle adopted, that of houses [a]round greens ... and the greens themselves arranged like the petals of a flower round a community building ...

Charles Reilly

The Reilly Plan

Reilly put forward a number of proposals, each using the same basic plan of grouping clusters of houses around a central green space with various communal facilities arranged in, on, and around the green. These included community centres, allotments, nursery facilities, communal kitchens and restaurants. In 1945 these ideas were expanded by Laurence Wolfe and published in *The Reilly Plan*. The book went into great detail on some of the possible variations of communal life that might be lived in the new settlements:

> *Ordinarily the young couple do not take a whole house, but one of the kitchenless 'bridal suites' provided in the village green, and they either feed at the community centre or have their meals delivered in an insulated container. This means that both husband and wife can go to work or continue their studies ... just as if they were unmarried, until the sixth or seventh month of the first pregnancy, which may occur within about two years of the marriage.*

Reilly drew up a number of schemes for Birkenhead, including a plan for the Woodchurch Estate and large-scale plan for the redevelopment of large parts of the town, all based on the concept of the 'Greens'. But in the end none of the plans were adopted by the Conservative-controlled council. It was left to others to champion the idea of communal housing estates. Reilly's plans were well received by some members of the architectural world. Clough Williams-Ellis, writing in *The Adventure of Building* in 1946 saw the proposals as an extension of the way that services such as electricity, roads and street lighting were already provided 'communally' and that Reilly's designs simply made it '... easy to extend this co-operation much further but in new and obviously sensible directions.' In December 1944 the Labour Party conference passed a motion approving Reilly's 'ideas for community planning.' In 1945 he was asked to draw up plans for the redevelopment of the Black Country town of Bilston. Despite having more support from the local council, his scheme was not taken forward.

A further plan was drawn up to house workers at the Miles Aircraft factory on the Woodley Airfield, near Reading; this also remained unbuilt. Eventually a modified version of the 'Greens' concept was built by Dudley Council in the late 1940s. The area, now known as 'The Greens', consists of a dozen open green

The Reilly Plan Layout plan of Reilly Greens from:
The Reilly Plan 1945

spaces surrounded by houses with a limited amount
of more conventional 'community facilities' such as
shops and schools located nearby.

By the 1960s it seems all knowledge of these early
schemes had faded and a new wave of people attracted
to communal living would have to (re)invent models
for themselves. Some of the communities that were set
up during the late 60s and early 70s have elements very
similar to cohousing. Places like Postlip Hall, Canon
Frome and Old Hall all have ownership models that
are precursors to those now being used by cohousing
groups and some are now even starting to 'rebrand'
themselves as cohousing. They all provide private space
for members and a variety of common shared facilities.
However, being in large country houses they tend to
lack the conscious design for informal socialisation
that characterised the early Scandinavian cohousing
and, it must be said, much of the co-operative housekeeping movement. In many ways the country house
architecture fights against the whole idea of communal
living, having been conceived to serve a hierarchical
social order. Though, having said that, it does provide
a sort of front-of-house area that lends itself to being

Proposed layout plan for Reilly Greens, Bilston

common facilities, and more human-scale servant quarters that are easier to convert to individual units.

The parallels between Co-operative Housekeeping and Cohousing are uncannily close – whether current groups have anything to learn from the schemes listed above would require more detailed research into both the design aspects of the individual schemes and the success, or not, of their social arrangements.

Google Earth view of The Greens, Dudley

Notes

A version of this article appears in: *Utopia Britannica: British Utopian Experiments 1325 -1945*. Chris Coates, Diggers & Dreamers Publications (2001)

The history of the co-operative housekeeping movement is told in: *The Architectural and Social History of Co-operative Living*. Lynn F. Pearson, Macmillan Press (1988). Out of Print.

1   Photos of Homesgarth are from *The Garden City - A Study in the Development of a Modern Town* by C B Purdom, (1913). Out of print, but may be viewed at:
www.archive.org/details/gardencitystudyi00purd

Chris Coates
is an editor of Diggers & Dreamers, a Green Party councillor and a member of Forgebank

View along shared / semi-private front spaces, Cambridge, Boston

Cohousing Evolution in Scandinavia and the USA

LUCY SARGISSON

Cohousing began in Demark and has flourished over the past twenty years in America. It stems from a criticism of contemporary urban life, which is viewed as isolating and alienating and it seeks to rebuild degraded communities.

Cohousing began in Denmark in the 1960s since when it has spread, grown and changed. This chapter explores some of these changes. National cohousing associations now exist across the world and particularly in Northern Europe, North America and Australasia: Britain (www.cohousing.org.uk); Denmark (www.xn--bofllesskab-c9a.dk)[1]; Sweden (www.kollektivhus.nu); Holland (www.lvcw.nl); USA (www.cohousing.org/directory); Canada (www. cohousing.ca); New Zealand (www.converge.org.nz/evcnz); and Australia (www.communities.org.au). Communities have recently been established in France (www.habitatgroupe.org) and Italy (www.cohousing. it). And while growth across much of Northern Europe was steady throughout the 1970s, 1980s and 1990s, in North America it began in the 1990s and has grown exponentially[2]. In February 2011, for example, The Federation of Intentional Communities listed 463 groups in its international directory which identify with cohousing principles. Four hundred of these were American. And the Cohousing Association of the United States listed 225 cohousing groups in the USA, of which 99 were fully formed (ie site purchased, building completed and members in residence).

There seem to be at least two different forms of cohousing. The first started in Nordic Europe and the second has spread across North America. Other scholars have noted this. For example, in 1991, Dorrit Fromm visited a cluster of new cohousing groups in the USA and found them to be quite different from the European model. These were less 'political' than the European communities, more interested in quality of life, private ownership and security. Their members sought safe places for their families to live in and were not concerned with wider issues of social/political change (Fromm, 1991). And in 2005, Jo Williams used the vocabulary of 'waves' to distinguish between these two different kinds of cohousing (Williams, 2005)[3]. My own research suggests that there is definitely something distinctive about contemporary American cohousing. For example, in continental Europe, cohousing communities almost always combine rented and privately owned homes (and some are all-rented). This is less common in North America, where the bias is towards owner-occupation. In mainland Europe, some cohousing communities are state-financed (forming part of state social housing policy). This is never the case in the USA or Canada.

I am concerned about over-generalising contemporary cohousing and there are significant differences between British and American cohousing (British cohousing is often more political). But what I want to do in this paper is to explore the new and fast-growing form of cohousing that has emerged across the United States over the last 20 years. In order to do this I have conducted a survey of 50 existing cohousing communities across the USA. The findings of this survey are reported below. First though, I offer brief summaries of the different sources of inspiration in Europe and the USA. I then offer a detailed discussion of contemporary American cohousing, which is structured through their criticisms of wider society, common structures and practices and finally shared values. Discussion concludes with a brief summary which asks, is this a radical phenomenon?

Different sources of inspiration

European cohousing had radical roots. The work of Bodil Graae and Jan Gudmand-Høyer was deeply political. Graae's article, 'Children Should Have One Hundred Parents', was explicitly feminist: it challenged the nuclear family and single-family households and argued for a radical transformation of the home.

Gudmand-Høyer's essay 'The Missing Link between Utopia and the Dated One-Family House' was firmly utopian: critical of the present and imagining a better world. He experimented with a new form of housing and saw this as a step along the road to a better world. Both of these activists believed that cities in the 1960s created isolation and alienation and that urban housing played a causal role. They sought practical solutions to these problems, attempting to restore 'disintegrating' community values, by creating better families and 'villages' in an urban context. They drew on feminist and communitarian values and they attempted to realise their desires through practical experimentation: Gudmand-Høyer's account of his attempt to set up a collective living experiment[4] is cited as direct inspiration for the first cohousing communities, Saettedammen and Skraplanet (1972/3), which still exist today.

Internal 'street' and sitting area, Jydstrup, Sjaelland, Denmark

In America, the roots of cohousing are anti-radical. They draw heavily on the works of Kathyrn McCamant and Charles Durrett, which are deeply pragmatic and anti-ideological. For example, they explicitly distance cohousing from other forms of collective living like this:

> *Cohousing ... differs from intentional communities and communes. Communes are often organized around strong ideological beliefs. Most intentional communities function as educational or spiritual centers. Cohousing, on the other hand, offers a new*

approach to housing rather than a new way of life. Based on democratic principles, cohousing developments espouse no ideology other than the desire for a more practical and social home environment'
(McCamant and Durrett, 1991: 1)

When they say, 'we are not ideological', McCamant and Durrett imply, 'we do not radically oppose the status quo'. When they say, 'we are practical and pragmatic' they imply 'we are not political'. I will explore these claims in the discussions that follow.

Cohousing practitioners' social criticism
My research suggests high levels of cohesion when it comes to social critique. This occurs across North America and also mainland Europe, the UK, New Zealand and Australia. When it comes to the question of what's wrong with modern society, cohousing national associations, networks and individual communities all identify similar things: the organisation of housing in modern towns and cities contributes to a lack of 'community', social deprivation, isolation and a waste of human capital (or potential).

Modern life means neighbours often don't recognise each other and day-to-day collaboration is minimal. Research has shown that 65% of people have nobody with whom they can co-operate in

Street view, Amherst, Mass., US

their daily lives and 84% don't have close relationships with their neighbours.* One in three people live alone, rising to 44% of older women.** When people are asked what concerns them most about the area they live, they highlight crime and antisocial behaviour, dirty streets, neglected open spaces, lighting and lack of facilities for young people.***
(UK Cohousing Network, 2008: 3)[5]

Urban life is depicted as alienated, un-neighbourly and making inefficient use of human potential. These broad sentiments are echoed in the public statements of individual communities across North America. For example:

Cohousing communities balance the traditional advantages of home ownership with the benefits of shared common facilities and ongoing connections with your neighbors. It attempts to overcome the alienation of modern subdivisions in which no one knows their neighbors, and there is no sense of community.
(Sonora Cohousing
sonoracoho.com/about_us
accessed 19.03.2010)

Cohousing is a way to live in community. We own our own homes and can find quiet and privacy there. But we also share many aspects of our lives – gardening, cooking, eating, celebrating and even raising our children together. Begun in Denmark, cohousing is a remarkable way to have fuller lives, a conscious effort to break the isolation that has become the hallmark of so many American neighbourhoods.
(Puget Ridge Cohousing
www.pugetridge.net
accessed 20.02.2010)

These extracts suggest a problem of social isolation – a situation in which neighbours are unfamiliar and people have few close relationships in their immediate location. Other people who live in the district are regarded as 'strangers', with mistrust and suspicion. Public spaces become spaces of feared or actual violence. There is little (or no) co-operation or civic responsibility and few opportunities for these to develop. There is, in short, no sense of collective belonging or 'community'. Instead, there are atomised individual residents, fearful of one another, high profile anti-social behaviour, neglected public spaces, and disaffected youth. This, they suggest, is both undesirable and unsustainable. In contrast, cohousing communities seek to offer viable alternatives and claim to 'stand as innovative answers to today's environmental and social problems' (US Cohousing Association, www.cohousing.org, accessed 28.01.10)

Common structures and values in American cohousing

The following discussion draws on data collected in a survey of North American cohousing communities conducted between January and March 2010. Samples for this survey were selected from members of the CoHousing Association of the United States, and include examples from each state with random selection within each state. Of the 99 existing communities belonging to this organisation, 50 were included in the survey. Thirty-four of the communities were urban, eight rural and eight self-described as 'sub-urban'[6]. Their size ranged from 7 to 50 households. The survey involved a simple form of content analysis, beginning with a close reading of the self-descriptions by each of the fifty groups on the national association website (www.cohousing.org). These are all written by a member of the community (ie not by a member of the association's staff)[7].

The survey revealed significant cohesion, showing a set of common values, structures and highly-valued behaviours and attitudes. While there are (of course) differences across (and within) individual communities, these do, I suggest, form part of a shared conception of community. And community is the primary goal of this form of cohousing. The first set of findings shows common structural features as follows:

Ninety-eight percent of all the groups in the sample mention commonly-owned facilities and the collective ownership of land and/or buildings. And most groups describe their physical site in some detail, which is intentionally designed to facilitate social interaction. There are two significant aspects to this: the design process itself and outcomes of that process.

The design itself is hugely consequential and shapes a large part of the cohousing experience. This includes factors such as the layout of roads, paths and outdoor space (gardens, orchards, play areas); location of parking areas, homes, community buildings and other

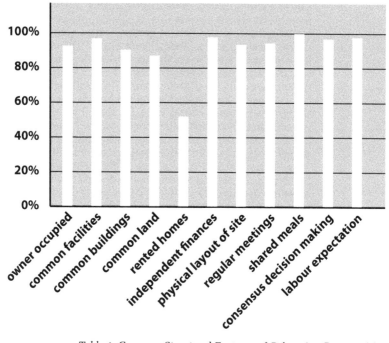

Table 1: Common Structural Features of Cohousing Communities

premises; and construction of the actual buildings (materials such as wood, straw-bale, rammed earth or brick), layout (how many storeys? how many rooms per home? which rooms are orientated in which direction?), and heating (such as passive solar, photovoltaics, or thermal ground source). All have an impact:

> *Residents have many opportunities to meet one another while they're getting their mail at the common house, strolling on the pedestrian walkway on which the houses all front, playing outdoors with their kids or their dogs, or walking to their cars. Because the center of the community is a pedestrian area, kids have a safe place to play away from cars.*
> (Shadow Lake Village, Virginia
> www.shadowlakevillage.org
> accessed 20.01.2010)

The survey also revealed common economic and social structures. For example, none of these groups are income-sharing and members retain independent finances. And all groups in the sample mentioned some features of intentional social design for 'community'.

These include social diversity (selecting members to achieve mixed generations, single-couple-family groups, ethnic and/or racial groups), shared meals, regular meetings and a 'labour commitment'. The latter is really important. The commitment to work (without remuneration) is presented as an act of citizenship within the group. People often evoke the vocabulary of empowerment, personal satisfaction and gaining new skills. The commitment to work for the community is common to both first and second wave cohousing. It was mentioned in 98% of the survey sample and occurs across all of the older European communities. This is a formal and contractual undertaking and it forms part of the tenancy/ownership contract, which normally specifies a number of hours expected from each adult member per month. The nature of work varies and examples include babysitting, preparing a community meal, gardening, book-keeping, taking older members shopping, dealing with visitor enquiries and building maintenance. In interview, members spoke about the satisfaction of working together, the social benefits and also (with some surprise) of the relationship between input and return: (for example, one individual spoke of contributing just a few hours a month but receiving a disproportionate return of twice-weekly meals in the common house, a weekly supply of fresh produce from the gardens and having their children collected from school each day).

The following extract is a typical expression of the aims of social design in cohousing communities:

Our vision is to create and sustain an urban community for 27 households in the Jackson Place neighborhood of Seattle. Our goal is to create an environment that nourishes a vibrant, meaningful life for every member, "providing individuals and families with what they need from a private point of view while allowing them to get what they want from a community point of view." ... As the residents, we are the designers, developers, and caretakers of our community. Community work is shared by all residents, and we gather in regular meetings to shape our direction and growth. We are committed to a consensus decision-making process. We strive to create an atmosphere of co-operation and goodwill where everyone is willing to lend a helping hand. We choose to develop relationships with each other based on mutual respect, trust, and honest communication. We agree to explore and

*to resolve, to the best of our ability, the inevitable
conflicts and misunderstandings that occur between
people living in community.*
(Jackson Place Cohousing Vision Statement
www.seattlecohousing.org/Vision.html
accessed 17.03.2010)

A second set of findings identified highly valued
behaviours and attitudes which are associated with a
'good community' (see Table on page 33):

Inside of dining area, Cambridge, Boston, US

Some terms require clarification. 'Sharing' refers to
the use of resources, facilities, space, time, energy and
activities. For example: 'We share goods and resources,
such as tools, transportation, child care, community-
supported agriculture, and common meals' (Jackson
Place CoHousing www.seattlecohousing.org/Vision.
html accessed 20.01.2010). 'Participation' is both
factored into membership (via residency agreements)
and indentified as a key to community success. And
'mutuality' is connected to the insistence by 65%
of the sample upon a balance between privacy and
community and the mention in 48% of cases of 'the
individual'.

It is important for these people that the 'giving' aspects
of community life should be reciprocal, that the active
participant in these communities should be able to
retreat into a private space and that nurture should
apply to both the individual and the collective. This
is not primarily a collective endeavour. Rather, partici-
pants stress the value of cohousing to the individual.

Evaluation: is American cohousing radical?

The survey supports the findings of other researchers, like Dorrit Fromm, who found a more individualistic form of cohousing in the USA, a version of the American Dream. Fromm expressed regret about this and I reserve judgement on this issue, but I do want to note two things. Firstly, cohousing is significant and it does work. These are 'better communities', their members feel that they are achieving their goals of a more supportive, neighbourly way of life with lower social exclusion and fear of violence. And studies by social scientists have revealed higher levels of citizenship and civic participation in cohousing than in conventional housing schemes (see Poley & Stephenson, 2007). Secondly, this form of cohousing is not radical. It is creative (for example, it works creatively around existing ideology and law), but it is not radical: it does not seek to overturn these. I am going to explore this briefly below.

Property is all about relationships and power: about discourses that tell us who we are and what rights we hold over things, places and people. And ownership consists of a complex series of relationships, which occur in the context of wider power relationships – for example, between the owner and the owned, between individual owners and between owner/s and the state. Overshadowing these are other, even wider sets of relationship, for example, between labour and capital, west and east, north and south. Cohousing narratives do not refer to these relationships but they are nonetheless embedded within them.

The western tradition of private ownership has a long history and is deeply embedded within discourses of the individual, including self ownership and self realisation. In these accounts, property is a sort of extension of the individual self, who is enmeshed in an epic struggle against other selves for recognition, autonomy or separation. The ownership of things confirms our existence. And the primary function of government is to protect our property[8]. I am not sanctioning these beliefs, just noting that they inform liberal ideology. Legal, sanctioned property rights, enforceable (by violence) with the legitimate might of the state, thus become part of the individual's armoury against other individuals. These ideas about property go a long way beyond the scope of cohousing but I note them because they silently inform many cultural assumptions and form the (unacknowledged) conceptual backdrop to

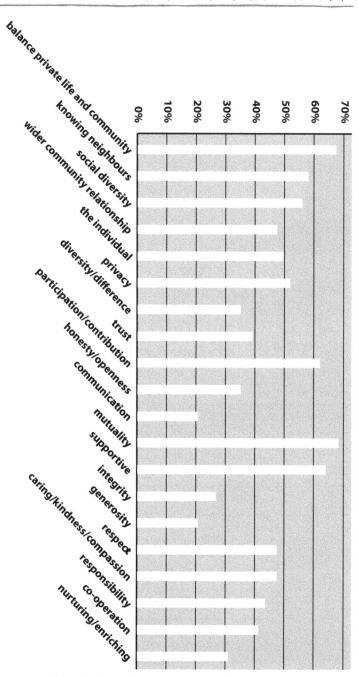

Table 2: Values, Behaviours and Attitudes

the cohousing assumptions about individual and collective ownership.

It is conventional, for example, to assume that ownership of a thing gives the possessor liberty over it ('it is mine, an extension of me and I may therefore do with it as I please'). At the same time, it is also conventional to assume that people will look after things they own ('this is mine and I therefore look after it'). What happens then, when people own things collectively? This is a

Street view, Greater Copenhagen, showing a blend of mainstream and cohousing properties; cohousing on the right

huge topic and I cannot do it justice here but, briefly, within this (liberal) conceptual paradigm of individual ownership it follows that people will not look after things that they do not own individually. What results is called the tragedy of the commons (Hardin, 1968) in which rational individual utility-maximisers ultimately spoil the common for all. American cohousing does not challenge this view. Instead it seeks to work around it. By extending private ownership to a collectively owned piece of land, cohousing seeks to preserve the benefits of private ownership while avoiding the tragedy of the commons. Simply put: they believe that owning something together means that people will look after it, together. Hence the collectively owned spaces. Members suggest that these 'common grounds' form a focus for collective activity, energy, commitment and communication. For example: 'Our attractive community hall is used often, for meetings, shared meals 2-3 times a week, parties, workshops, rehearsals, slide shows, concerts, and meetings. We know our neighbors and help each other out in many ways' (Rosewind CoHousing, www.cohousing.org/directory/view/2046, accessed 17.02.2010).

In the American cohousing narrative, shared ownership of a semi-public space (ie public within the community) constitutes a 'common wealth', a social resource and a social good. To achieve this end, cohousing takes advantage of the fact that the ownership of land permits certain (sanctioned) freedom or autonomy within the boundaries of the owned space (see Carruthers & Ariovich, 2004). This is not a free licence or an unbounded right or a total autonomy and it is restricted by national and local property rules and other prior relationships (DeFilippis, 1999). However, it does give a certain freedom. It permits the opportunity and the right to develop and shape this space. Of course, this applies to all owners and not just collective ones, but it has special significance in a collective context. Here, the group participates in the design process and the collective ownership of land permits the group intentionally to shape and develop it together. And this collective shaping of physical space is an important part of the cohousing story.

This has positive outcomes and the efficacy and impact of architectural design have been much-studied (see, for example, Williams, 2005, Marcus & Sarkissan, 1986, and Marcus & Dovey, 1991). This is a vast topic and I cannot do it justice but I will note three points by way of illustration. New-build cohousing communities share certain physical and architectural features and traits. Firstly, homes are often clustered around common spaces (garden, orchard, or 'village green'). This addresses issues of quality of life (allowing all residents the pleasure not only of owning open space but also of seeing this from their homes). It also addresses issues of anti-social behaviour (permitting casual surveillance of this space by all neighbours). Secondly, domestic units (houses and flats) tend to be small in cohousing settlements. This is deliberate. It is argued that because they share common facilities, households need less private space in cohousing than in other housing projects (McCamant & Durrett, 1988). Residents have rights of access and use over shared functional and leisure facilities (such as laundries and gardens) and do not need large homes. They are thus encouraged (through push and pull factors) to spend less time alone in their homes and more in semi-public spaces (community library, pool or gym) (Williams, 2005). Thirdly, these are highly pedestrianised spaces. Most have a common parking area (close to the most public edge of the collectively owned space) and footpaths that lead residents past each other's homes, which are adjacent to wide walkways. People walk to and from the parking areas, meeting each other along the way. These are just three examples of physical design features that facilitate 'interaction' within cohousing units, manipulating human activity through the organisation of space.

Of course, architects could (and do) attempt this without collective ownership (see, for example, New Urbanism, a commercial architectural approach which seeks to facilitate community[9]). However, the fact that this land is owned by the group and also that the first generation of residents have participated in the design is significant. Owning the site together gives members collective rights to shape and organise its layout in such a way that will eventually shape their own behaviour. Doing so collectively and with deliberate intent makes the organisation of space a matter of empowerment for cohousing members.

So American cohousing does not challenge the dominant ideology or practice of ownership. It does not seek to end private ownership of property, for example. Nor does it practise communal living. But it does believe that owning some land collectively and organising physical space deliberately and carefully can facilitate better communities. It is effective but not radical. It is, I think, ideological but this is a conventional liberal western ideology and not an oppositional one. It is in many ways consistent with the American Dream.

And it is popular: people like it and more people are trying it every year. New groups appear on the websites of cohousing national associations each month and the conversion rate from 'aspired' to 'realised' community has increased. In part, this is because mainstream funders and planners have started to support it, albeit cautiously. It is possible to gain funding from 'highstreet' lenders for cohousing developments and named funders in the survey included the National Bank of Arizona, Evergreen Bank, Exchange Bank, Wells Fargo, Luther Burbank, and Horizon Bank. This would not be possible if it were identified as a radical or oppositional movement.

So, what might be the lessons from all this for the UK cohousing movement? Firstly, the American experience shows that cohousing offers a blueprint for better communities. We know this already because Britain already has its own thriving cohousing groups. But (secondly) the American experience suggests that it could be more widely practised. It suggests that cohousing offers many benefits to its members and to the local neighbourhood and that it is not necessary to be radical, or even politically motivated, to benefit from this. It adapts existing property rules to shape space and influence human behaviour in such a way as to develop better communities (and better individuals). This could be a useful message for British cohousing. Thirdly, and this will be familiar to cohousing practitioners but it's worth mentioning nonetheless, cohousing works only because it is genuinely participatory. The facts that members co-design their homes and co-design the rules that shape their interactions are essential. Cohousing is not something that can be imposed from the top down (for example by local or national governments). But, fourthly, because it works and because it is not oppositional, it might be of interest to these bodies. Perhaps UK authorities could be encouraged by the American experience to view planning applications more sympathetically.

Part of me might regret the lack of radicalism in American cohousing but I do think that this accounts for the speed of its growth. By distancing itself from radical social movements that seek to overthrow the system, American cohousing practitioners have been able to secure funding and building/planning consents for their schemes.

The older European version certainly articulated communitarian values and was located within broader projects for radical change. But American cohousing is different: it does not reject capital, or property, or power. It is not going to completely change the world and that is not its intention. Instead, it seeks to provide better, safer, more participatory communities and to develop better people, who are more 'empowered'; possessed of complex social skills, socially literate, regularly participating in their local community and exercising some control over it. It is explicitly (sometimes dogmatically) pragmatic and this makes it widely transferrable, so that it provides a malleable framework, accessible to social conservatives as well as to radicals. So, for example, it could appeal to Conservative Party advocates of a so-called 'Big Society' as well as Green Party activists. This is not unproblematic, ethically or ideologically, but it might be useful if the British cohousing movement wants to grow.

(All photos in this chapter courtesy Martin Field)

References – Books and Articles

- CARRUTHERS, B.C. & ARIOVICH, L (2004). 'The Sociology of Property Rights' in *Annual Review of Sociology* Vol 30: 23-46.

- DEFILIPPIS, J (1999). 'Alternatives to the "New Urban Politics": finding locality and autonomy in local economic development' in *Political Geography*, Vol 18: 973-990.

- FIELD, M. (2004). *Thinking About Cohousing: the creation of intentional neighbourhoods* (London: Diggers & Dreamers Publications),

- FROMM, D. (1991). *Collaborative Communities: cohousing central living and other forms of housing with shared facilities* (New York: Van Nostrand Reinhold).

- GRAAE, B. (1967). 'Børn skal have Hundrede Foraeldre', Politiken (Copenhagen), April 1967.

- GUDMAND-HØYER, J. (1968). 'Det manglende led mellem utopi og det foraeldede en familiehus'. *Information* 26 June 1968.

- HARDIN, G. (1968). 'The Tragedy of the Commons' in *Science*, Vol 162,1243-1248.

- HARDY, D. (2006). *Poundbury: The Town that Charles Built* (London: Town and Country Planning Association).

- KATZ, PETER (1994) *The New Urbanism: toward an architecture of community* (New York: McGraw-Hill).

- KIM, G 'An Interview with Jan Gudmand-Høyer' www.cohousing.org/2009/prog/frikeynote, accessed 23.03.2010.

- LOCKE, J. (1689 [1960 edn]). *Two Treatises of Government* (Cambridge: CUP)

- MCCAMANT, K. & DURRETT, C, (1988). *Cohousing: A Contemporary Approach to Housing Ourselves* (Berkley, CA: Ten Speed Press).

- MCCAMANT, K. & DURRETT, C, (1991). 'Cohousing Communities: Sustaining Ourselves, Sustaining Our Communities' *Co-op America Quarterly* 13, Spring, at: www.ecovisionquest.com/cohousing.htm.

- MARCUS, C. & SARKISSAN (1986). *Housing as if people mattered: site design for medium density family housing* (Berkeley, CA: University of California Press).

- MARCUS, C. & DOVEY, K (1991). 'Cohousing: an option for the 1990s' *Progressive Architecture* Vol 6

- MELTZER, G. (2005). *Sustainable Community, learning from the cohousing model* (Victoria, BC: Trafford).

- POLEY, L. & STEPHENSON, M. (2007). 'Community and the Habits of Democratic Citizenship: An Investigation into Civic Engagement, Social Capital and Democratic Capacity-Building in U.S. Cohousing Neighborhoods' Paper prepared for the 103rd annual meeting of the American Political Science Association. Chicago, Illinois August 30 – September 2, 2007.

- PRINCE OF WALES, (1989). *A Vision of Britain: a personal view of architecture* (London: Doubleday).

- SAGUARO SEMINAR 'Social Capital National Benchmark Survey', Harvard University 2000-2006, www.hks.harvard.edu/saguaro/measurement/measurement.htm

- SCOTTHANSON, C. & SCOTTHANSON, K. (2005) *The Cohousing Handbook: building a place for better community* (Gabriola Island, CA New Society Publishers).

- WILLIAMS, J. (2005). 'Designing Neighbourhoods for Social Interaction: the case of cohousing' in *Journal of Urban Design* Vol 10, No2, 195-227.

- WILLIAMS, J. (2005a). 'Sun, surf and sustainable housing – cohousing, the Californian experience' *International Planning Studies* Vol 10, Issue 2: 145-177.

- UK COHOUSING NETWORK (2008). Annual Report.

Cohousing websites

Australian Cohousing Association
www.communities.org.au

British Cohousing Network
www.cohousing.org.uk

Canadian Cohousing Network
www.cohousing.ca

Dallas-Fort Worth Cohousing
www.dfwnetmall.com/ecovillage/
origins-cohousing-how-began.htm
accessed 19.03.2010.

Danish Cohousing Association
www.xn--bofllesskab-c9a.dk

EarthSong Cohousing, Waitakere, New Zealand
www.earthsong.org.nz

Great Oak Cohousing, Ann Arbour Michigan
www.gocoho.org/cohousing
accessed 19.04.2010

Italian Cohousing Association
www.cohousing.it

Jackson Place Cohousing, Seattle
www.seattlecohousing.org/Vision.html

Landelijke Vereniging Centraal Wonen
www.lvcw.nl

McCamant and Durrett Architects
www.mccamant-durrett.com

Melbourne Cohousing Network
home.vicnet.net.au/~cohouse

New Zealand Ecovillage & Cohousing Association
www.converge.org.nz/evcnz

Puget Ridge Cohousing, Seattle, Washington
www.pugetridge.net

Rosewind Cohousing, Port Townsend, Washington
www.cohousing.org/directory/view/2046

Shadow Lake Village, Blacksburg, Virginia
www.shadowlakevillage.org

Sonora Cohousing Community, Tucson, Arizona
www.sonoracohousing.com/coho/

Swedish Cohousing Network
www.kollektivhus.nu/

Sustainable Community Action Wiki
sca21.wikia.com/wiki/Cohousing
accessed 19.04.2010

Ten Stones Cohousing, Vermont
www.tenstones.info

United States Cohousing Association
www.cohousing.org

Notes

1. Approximately 1% of the Danish population live in cohousing (roughly 50,000 people).

2. For example, of 95 communities in the USA in 2009, 33 were completed during the 1990s and 59 during the 2000s www.cohousing.org/directory.

3. Some also identify a 'third wave' around the Pacific Rim, Australia and South East Asia.

4. His article was written following an unsuccessful attempt to create a collective housing community: working with a group of friends, Gudmand-Høyer purchased land and planned a housing development at Hareskov, outside Copenhagen, in 1964. The project was short-lived (owing to local opposition).

5. Internal references: * National Lifestyle Preferences. 2006, **General Household Survey 2005, and ***New Economics Foundation 2008.

6. ie, 'semi-rural'.

7. Some sections of these webpages are unstructured (free-form narratives) and some are structured around subheadings provided

by the association (on a pro forma). The latter are useful for comparability (for example, each group is asked to provide information on a number of factual areas such as labour expectations, decision-making procedures and form of ownership). In this exercise, a value of 1 was entered if a term was mentioned in either of these sections and the findings below are not weighted. A second stage of analysis involved visits to the individual community websites, where the same exercise was repeated (with no double-entering if the term was used twice). So the charts just tell us if the terms are used in North American cohousing community self-descriptions. This is, as noted above, a simple method of analysis but it does yield some interesting results, which are supplemented by discussions from qualitative readings of these texts.

8. See, for example, the work of John Locke, whose political theory strongly influenced the US Founding Fathers.

9. For examples of New Urbanist towns, see Poundbury, Dorset (www.poundbury.info) and Seaside, Florida (www.seasidefl.com) and above references Hardy, 2006; Prince of Wales, 1989; and Katz, 1994.

Lucy Sargisson
works in the University of Nottingham's School of Politics

Close Relationships: Learning from the Cohousing Model

GRAHAM MELTZER

This article comes from Graham's book Sustainable Community, Learning from the cohousing model *(Trafford Publishing, 2005) which is based on a ten-year study of twelve cohousing developments in Canada, the United States of America, New Zealand, Australia and Japan.*

B eing in relationship implies both *association* and *connection* between two or more entities[1]. In a cohousing context, association assumes an intentional or purposive guise, most overtly expressed through *sharing*. Given the potential in cohousing for the expression of caring, the connection between members and the bonding of the membership as a whole is most clearly expressed through *support*. *Sharing* and *support* are dimensions of their social *relationships* that cohousing members said had significantly enhanced their pro-environmental practices.

Sharing: defusing the consumerist imperative

To *share*, means to possess, use or occupy jointly with others, whereby some manner of give-and-take or reciprocity is implied[2]. Sharing is a defining feature of cohousing. It involves explicit or implicit agreements made by the group (or a subgroup of households) which enable efficiencies to be developed and mutual benefits to be derived. Sharing builds social relationships but is also dependent upon them, in that the degree to which residents are willing to share depends upon the trust and goodwill they have established.

Sharing in cohousing occurs in at least two ways:

- informal sharing between residents of their private possessions; and,

- formalised sharing of community-owned indoor and outdoor facilities and amenities.

"Having common laundry facilities makes me aware of doing frivolous loads of laundry as I have to share the space, time, work etc with others."

"Sharing things reduces the need for so much. Sharing can reduce consumption of resources and the time we spend on material things – freeing up time to do the things we would really like to do!"

"There's less consumerism in cohousing; it's easy to borrow things we don't have and to lend to neighbours things we have which they don't."

"We use community tools and appliances instead of having our own."

"We car-share instead of buying a new car. We rent half of a neighbour's."

"With like-minded people around a lot of resource sharing happens naturally."

Informal sharing

Discussion of sharing in the cohousing literature is often limited to use of the common house, the most visible expression of community-wide co-operation. Yet willingness to share and co-operate is pervasive in a viable community, as one cohousing resident explains:

> *A one-car family can always borrow another in a pinch instead of owning two. We often join forces and carpool on outings. We have three lawn-mowers instead of 25. Quite a few of us don't have TVs, but when the TV-less want to watch something special, there's always a willing neighbor who'd like the company. Very few of us have guest rooms, but one family's guests will often stay in the home of a neighbor who's away for the weekend[3].*

Cohousing lore holds that sharing reduces household consumption. It is supposed to enable each household to live in a smaller dwelling with fewer goods and with less need to buy items that they can share. One member notes, 'we're always lending each other our camping equipment, tools, books, videos, missing ingredients for a dish in progress, thus diminishing our consumer addictions and saving trips to the store'[4]. Items anecdotally said to be communally owned or readily shared include lawn mowers, garden equipment, carpentry tools, washers, dryers, freezers, televisions and video recorders.

Indeed the data supports this view, revealing a reduction in the quantities of some of these items per household. Residents were asked to report the numbers of certain items they owned before moving into cohousing and the change, if any, in that number since (see Table 1, particularly the final column). Responses revealed negligible change in the numbers of household refrigerators, televisions and dishwashers; a moderate (one quarter) reduction in the number of freezers, washing machines and dryers; and a significant (three quarters) reduction in the number of lawn mowers owned privately.

Item		Refrigerators	Televisions	Dishwashers	Freezers	Dryers	Washers	Mowers
Change in number owned per household	2 fewer	-	2	-	-	-	-	7
	1 fewer	22	35	40	31	82	79	122
	nil	230	204	195	238	176	183	148
	1 more	28	37	45	11	21	18	3
	2 more	-	1	-	-	1	-	-
	3 more	-	1	-	-	-	-	-
Net change		6	3	5	-20	-61	-61	-133
Total number owned		281	360	184	70	153	171	45
percentage change		2%	1%	3%	-22%	-29%	-26%	-75%

Table 1: Changes in household ownership of goods

An even greater benefit may well be derived from the ready sharing of smaller items. 'Before buying a consumer item we check first to see if someone here already has one we can use' comments one member. At least one community has operationalised this process by circulating a list of building, gardening, camping, cooking and other equipment that each household owns and is willing to share (Table 2). Members refer

Category	Item	Lender Unit #	Category	Item	Lender Unit #
Gardening	Hand trowel	A5,A6,B1,B4	Cleaning	Mini vacuum	A7,C4
	Lawn mower	A6		Rug cleaner	B1
	Leaf rake	A2,A5,A6,B1,B3	Outings	Backpack	A6,A7,B1,C7,D3
	Weed scythe	C4		Bicycle tools	A7,B1,C7,D3
	Wheelbarrow	A2,A4,A6,B1,C4		Car bike rack	A5,A6,B1,C5,C7
Building etc	Backbelt	A6,B1,B3		Maps	A6,B1,B4,C7,D4
	Bucket	CH,B1,B3		Snowshoes	D3
	Jigsaw	A6		Tents	A7,B1,B4,D2,D3
	Sewing machine	A6,B3,B4,C7,D3		Coffee pot	A6,D5
	Staple gun	A6,B1,C7	Oversize	Oversize mixer	CH,D4
	Toilet plunger	A5,B1	Other	Blow up bed	C4,D5
	Toilet snake	B1		Single futon	D5
Cooking	Wok	A6,B1,B4,D4		Folding tables	B1,D3,C6,C7

Table 2: Part (about a third) of a lending list of household items available to others[5].

to the list should they want to borrow an item and approach one of the relevant households.

There is enough evidence to suggest that the consumerist imperative that seems endemic in the West is significantly defused in cohousing. Cohousing residents are generally much less concerned with material acquisition – the size of their dwelling, the model of their car, the most fashionable clothing or the latest home entertainment system. They value consumer goods simply for their functionality, not their monetary worth or perceived fashionability. Especially during the first one or two years, cohousing communities commonly shed excessive quantities of duplicated consumer items that members no longer want or need (Photo 1).

Shared facilities
Shared facilities, such as those found in a typical common house, take considerable coordinated effort to operate and maintain. They represent the commitment of cohousing groups to the ideal of co-operation and are critical to social development and group cohesion. The extent and make-up of shared facilities varies widely in cohousing. Some communities have built multi-purpose, full-featured common houses and others more modest ones. Sometimes the indoor facilities are located in one building, the common house, though usually they are spread between two or more buildings. Table 3 is an inventory of existing

and proposed shared (indoor) facilities in each of the communities (at the end of 2003).

The list is ordered according to the 'count' of built facilities (2 points) and proposed but not yet built facilities (1 point) in each community. However, cross-community comparison on the basis of this data should be undertaken with great caution. There is complex reasoning behind a group's choice of common facilities. The size of the community, its demographic mix and financial capacity are obvious factors. In Tokyo, for example, economic and cultural factors have severely limited opportunities for dedicated shared space. Interpretation is further hampered by the incompleteness of some common facilities at the time of the evaluation. Earthsong Eco-Neighbourhood, for example, has been making do with a pre-existing farmhouse until its common house is built.

The columns of Table 3 are ordered according to the total 'count' of built and proposed facilities in all of the

Photo 1: Items left in the Swan's Market common house about to be redistributed or donated to a worthy cause. The notice on the wall reads:

- *Stuff Disposal Week -*
- *Sun-Tues: Take it if it's yours*
- *Wed-Sat: Take it whether or not it's yours*
- *Sunday: It goes to MOCHA's [nearby museum of Children's Art] white elephant sale!*

	Kitchen	Dining Area	Laundry	Social Space	Guest Room	Kids'Room	Workshop	Office	TV/VCR	Library	Games Room	Craft Room	Hot Tub/Pool	Exercise Room	Teens'Room	
WindSong Cohousing	••	••	••	••	••	••	••	••	••	••	••	••	•	••	••	29
Marsh Commons Cohousing	••	••	••	••	••	••	••	••	••	•	••	••	•			24
Puget Ridge Cohousing	••	••	••	••	••	••	••		••	•	••	•				20
Berkeley Cohousing	••	••	••	••	••	••	•	••	••	••						19
Songaia Cohousing	••	••	••	••	••	••	••	••					•		•	18
North Street Cohousing	••	••	••	••			••		••	••	••		••			18
Cascade Cohousing	••	••	••	••	••	••	••		••	••						18
Swan's Market Cohousing	••	••	••	••	••	••	••							•	••	17
Quayside Village Cohousing	••	••	••	••	••	••		••			••					16
Earthsong Eco-Neighbourhood	••	•	••	••	•	••	••	••		•					•	16
Cohousing Cooperative	••	••	••	••	••	•	•	••								14
Kyôdô no mori Cohousing	••	••														4
Total coun	24	23	22	22	19	19	18	14	12	11	8	7	6	4	4	

Table 3: Schedule of existing and proposed common facilities
[•• = built facilities, • = intended facilities]

groups evaluated. The ordering and banding suggest a prioritisation of common facilities, from those deemed essential (laundry, social space, kitchen and dining room) to those considered highly desirable (guest room, kids' room and workshop) and so on. Apart from the laundry, the most highly valued amenities are those associated with the development of social relationships. Groups appear to recognise the link between available amenity, the social interaction it engenders and the building of group cohesion. A most poignant outcome of the analysis, however, is the low importance attached to teenage facilities. This can no doubt be rationalised in communities with low numbers of teens but this finding supports anecdotal evidence for the needs of teenagers being poorly met in cohousing.

The area analysis offered in Table 4 is also revealing and to some extent addresses anomalies in the previous table such as the incomplete state of some common houses and the critical mass (related to community size) necessary for the viability of particular facilities. The measure, area of common space, includes all built facilities, not just those in the common house. Observation and anecdotal evidence suggest that communities with a high common to private space ratio enjoy and make good use of their common house but struggle to optimise its use. Those groups with low ratios of common to private space tend not to 'hang out' in the common house and are constrained by space limitations when the whole community comes together. The data suggests that a ratio of common to private space somewhere between 0.13 and 0.17 is optimal. Whilst not wanting to take the numerical analysis too far, it seems reasonable to suggest that a hypothetical 'average' cohousing community of 18 households should seek to build a common house of around 280m^2. The sharing of resources requires a considerable commitment of time and energy in

	Number of households	Area of common space (m2)	Common space per household (m2)	Average dwelling size (m2)	Ratio of common to private space
Marsh Commons Cohousing	17	418	25	105	0.24
Swan's Market Cohousing	20	465	23	95	0.24
Songaia Cohousing	13	325	25	127	0.20
Cascade Cohousing	15	280	19	101	0.19
Puget Ridge Cohousing	23	372	16	95	0.17
Quayside Village Cohousing	19	240	13	80	0.16
WindSong Cohousing	34	557	16	115	0.14
Berkeley Cohousing	14	169	12	87	0.14
Earthsong Eco-neighbourhood	17	200	12	92	0.13
Cooperative Cohousing	11	130	12	108	0.11
North Street Cohousing	17	170	10	110	0.09
Kyōdō no mori Cohousing	12	25	2	90	0.02
Mean	18	280	15	100	0.15

Table 4: Area analysis of common versus private space.

cleaning, maintenance, improvement and management. All groups start with the premise that everyone who is able should contribute a certain amount of time in their 'civic duty' to make the community successful. However, the method by which groups get the work done varies widely, with each group evolving a different arrangement over many years. Some groups maintain a loose, informal understanding, while others strictly regulate and monitor the relative contribution of their members. In some communities individual members sign up for particular tasks but in most places groups or teams take responsibly for a building, an area of the property or a package of tasks.

"There's plenty of support – emotional and practical – for environmental views"

"Simple things happen, like a neighbour's trip to the grocery store turns into picking up milk for me (that's one less trip)"

"The community supports ecological practices naturally and encourages the children to do so"

"Cohousing offers significant support to a simpler more sustainable lifestyle"

"Cohousing supports my efforts to live closer to what I believe is right"

Support: restoring 'traditional' personal relationships
In their influential book, *Habits of the Heart*, the authors (Robert Bellah *et al.*) characterise 'classic' or 'traditional' personal relationships as those with three principal dimensions: *social*, *practical*, and *moral*. Good friends, they argue, must:

- value one another's company (ie enjoy social support);

- be useful to one another (ie provide practical support); and

- share a commitment to the common good (ie effect moral support).

They suggest that all three aspects have been suppressed in contemporary Western society. Such 'habits of the heart', they argue, 'made sense more readily in the small face-to-face communities that characterised early American society'[6].

Yet, it is *exactly* this tripartite social relationship that is the norm in cohousing.

1 Social support – diminished in contemporary society through reduced propinquity – is restored in cohousing through ready-found 'caring and sharing'.

2 Practical support is ubiquitous in cohousing through close-knit neighbouring.

3 Moral support is the collective consciousness in cohousing that maintains support for, and validation of, individual members by the group.

Many cohousing residents report that the support of friends, neighbours and the community at large is the single greatest influence upon their environmental practices.

Social support
While most cohousing residents have intimate relationships with one or a few unrelated others with whom they can share personal problems, communities recognise that not all members are so connected. Hence, men's, women's and parent's support groups are common. Some cohousing communities have a committee for the purpose of addressing the personal needs of their members. Radically changed circumstance and emergency situations are often the catalyst for such support. Loss of employment may trigger a loan from an emergency support fund. Accommodation within the community will be found for one of a couple undergoing separation. A cooking roster may be developed to provide meals for a family in need. A single mother, for example, reported not having to cook for two months after the birth of her child.

Social support can be critically important in times of tragedy, trauma or dire need. In one community, the 'Caring and Sharing Committee' wrote a page-long article in their newsletter describing the plight of a member suffering Alzheimer's Disease and his carer-partner. They recommended a long list of ways in which members could assist the couple: keeping in touch, calling by, running errands, offering to give the carer a break, taking them out, offering companionship, getting involved etc. The potential for this kind of deep, therapeutic caring and support is inherent within small-scale communal societies, as Rosbeth Kanter has famously documented.

> In many ways the intense love and care, the close coordination of production and consumption, the participation in and sharing of power, the integration of home and work, and the elimination of private property often characteristic of fully developed utopian communities makes them well suited to attacking problems of therapy[7].

Practical support

Practical support in cohousing can occur in countless ways. There is willingness to care for their garden or feed their cat when neighbours take a vacation. Ready advice is given and time spent helping neighbours to install new software, fix a leaky faucet or move heavy furniture. Such mutual aid can save money, alleviate stress and imbue relationships with substance. It is an essential ingredient of the 'social glue' of most cohousing communities.

Practical support is probably best illustrated by informal childcare. In cohousing, the amenity and safety of common open space and the close proximity of children of similar ages elevates outdoor play beyond watching television as most kids' preferred pastime. Parental willingness to let children play freely outdoors is only possible, however, with the tacit support of a significant proportion of the rest of the community. Knowing that adults are somewhere around, that an informal neighbourhood watch is being kept on the commons and that other houses are open to their kids offers parents a peace of mind that is rare in contemporary society.

Having relationships of trust with a number of close neighbours enables parents to spontaneously, or by regular arrangement, trade baby-sitting and childcare duties. This can be invaluable for single parents. At one community, for instance, a midwife called to duty at 2 am knows she can call a neighbour who will immediately come and sleep over with her children. Retired members of many communities and those working at home become surrogate parents, feeding neighbours' kids after school and supervising their play until parents return from work. The elderly become surrogate grandparents. The community becomes a surrogate family.

To a large extent, the availability of such support depends on the diversity of work circumstances and lifestyles. It requires that not all adults commute to 9-to-5 jobs. As previously noted, cohousing has considerable diversity of this kind. Only 50% of adults work full-time. Those employed part-time comprise 22%; full-time students comprise 11% and homemakers 5% of the adult population. Another 5% are retired, 4% are unemployed and 4% have independent means of support. A considerable proportion of residents spend significant amounts of time at home. Sixteen percent make their living from home on either a full-time or part-time basis and about 20% more are based at home as students, homemakers, unemployed or retired.

Moral support
Whether it features in a mission statement or not, all cohousing groups agonise over matters of *equity*, with some members suggesting that it is one of '*the three 'e's of sustainability*' along with environment, and economics. Equity is taken here to mean 'the common good' or the even-handed treatment of all, and in particular, community support for the needs of minorities. Gays and lesbians, for example, have found cohousing to be a haven from homophobia and discrimination. Two lesbian mothers once wrote in their community newsletter, 'cohousing ... offered a safe, nurturing environment for our "alternative" – we like to think normal – family. We are free to be ourselves here and feel accepted as a family'[8].

In practice, however, real equity proves as difficult to achieve in cohousing as it does elsewhere. Wheelchair access to at least some units is possible in most projects but only a few (eg Quayside Village and WindSong) have purpose-built ground floor units with full and easy accessibility. Almost all common houses are on two levels, making disabled access to some facilities impossible or difficult. Notably, where disabled members have joined the group during a project's development phase, greater effort has been made to meet their needs. At one community, for instance, the involvement of a disabled child during development of the project resulted in all units being made wheelchair accessible so that he could freely visit his friends.

Such consideration is very rare however as only about 2% of the cohousing population have a serious physical or intellectual disability. This is undoubtedly an issue which could be better addressed in future cohousing projects — as a means of 'future-proofing' dwellings against aging if not as a show of moral support for disabled visitors. Even more difficult to accommodate are the needs of members with ailments such as hypersensitivity to chemicals and synthetics. Whilst they and other residents concerned with indoor air quality can specify benign materials and finishes within their own dwellings, such consideration is not often extended to the common house.

Affordability
Housing affordability is also considered as a matter of equity. Cohousing groups equate entry-level access to cohousing with moral support for less wealthy members. Against a background (during the 1980s and '90s) of unparalleled decline in housing affordability,

	Project cost (all in US$)	Number of dwellings	Average dwelling Cost (US$)	Average dwelling size (m2)	Average dwelling cost per m2 (US$)
Cohousing Cooperative	$720,000	11	$65,455	108	$606
Cascade Cohousing	$1,360,000	15	$90,667	101	$898
WindSong Cohousing	$3,800,000	34	$111,765	115	$972
North Street Cohousing	$1,960,000	17	$115,294	110	$1,048
Marsh Commons Cohousing	$2,540,000	17	$149,412	105	$1,423
Puget Ridge Cohousing	$3,350,000	23	$145,652	95	$1,533
Earthsong Eco-Neighbourhood	$2,400,000	17	$141,176	92	$1,535
Quayside Village Cohousing	$2,400,000	19	$126,315	79	$1,599
Songaia Cohousing	$2,700,000	13	$207,692	127	$1,635
Berkeley Cohousing	$2,580,000	14	$184,286	87	$2,118
Swan's Market Cohousing	$5,260,000	20	$263,000	95	$2,768
Kyōdō no mori Cohousing	$5,500,000	12	$458,333	90	$5,093
Mean	$2,880,833	18	$171,587	100	$1,769

Table 5: Cohousing affordability analysis.

founding members of every group said they had aspired to relative affordability and strove to keep base-level housing costs as low as possible. Groups minimised dwelling size and standardised or replicated house design. Some groups limited customisation on the assumption that varying the design for individual households would increase costs for the whole community. Other strategies included infrastructure rationalisation, design for adaptive reuse and the use of recycled materials.

Yet it seems that cohousing is still not particularly affordable. Table 5 offers a basic analysis of the cost of entering cohousing. Total project cost has been divided by the number of dwellings in each community to produce an average dwelling cost. This is then divided by the average dwelling size to produce an average dwelling cost per m^2. Once again, this kind of analysis must be treated with caution. Fine-grained analysis by location and household income would be necessary before firm conclusions could be drawn about housing affordability. However, the raw data is still revealing.

The first four projects could be said to be genuinely 'affordable'. Australian cohousing, in particular, has achieved a remarkable level of affordability. Cohousing Co-operative would be the most affordable project of all, but is almost fully government funded anyway. Their successful cost minimisation can be attributed to a strictly limited budget, efficient replicated architectural design and very tight construction management – all of which is more likely with a publicly funded project. Cascade Cohousing utilised sweat equity to good affect. To some extent both projects reaped cost benefits due to location. Real estate values and the cost of construction are lower in Hobart than elsewhere in Australia.

The Windsong Cohousing project enjoyed excellent economies of scale and the cost advantages of close clustering and innovative project management[9]. North Street Cohousing demonstrates the cost advantages of retrofit cohousing, although this project also benefited from its location in a low-cost neighbourhood. At the other end of the scale, the Tokyo project starkly reflects the distorted real estate values in that city. Similarly, Berkeley Cohousing and Swan's Market illustrate the extent of real estate inflation in the Bay area.

The remaining projects can be said to be more typical of cohousing generally. Homeowners in these communities paid, on average, US $ 154,000 to join the project. The prices include a share of the commons, of course, which delivers enormous lifestyle advantages. Therefore, comparison with regular housing costs should be highly qualified. The projects were all constructed in the mid 1990s when the national median house price in the US and Canada was around US $ 150,00010. Based on these figures, it seems that cohousing is no more affordable than regular housing, possibly less so. This is a salutary finding given that cohousing is commonly misconceived or misrepresented as a means to affordable housing. The data suggests that it most definitely is not.

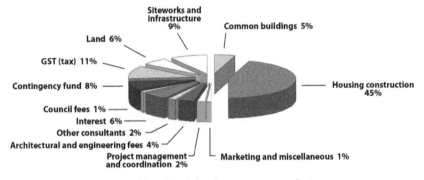

Figure 1: Earthsong Eco-Neighbourhood development cost analysis (Analysis by Peter Scott)

One reason for cohousing sometimes being even less affordable than typical family housing is the complexity of the development process and the number of consultants involved. This is well illustrated in the project development cost analysis produced for Earthsong Eco-Neighbourhood (Figure 1). Note that the cost of construction of the dwellings alone amounts to just 45% of the total whilst the so-called 'soft costs' (ie consultants' fees, taxes, administrative costs etc.) comprise more than a quarter of the total budget.

In recognition of the challenge of affordability, support for low-income members is provided in a number of cohousing communities. A few, including Quayside, WindSong and Berkeley, have successfully raised government subsidies for some units. Others have arranged extra financial assistance from investment companies. Some groups have assisted lower income members with internal loans, subsidies and sliding-scale contribution schemes (for condominium and body corporate fees). Most simply seek to provide rental accommodation for those who can't afford to buy into the community. North Street, for example, with 20 renters in a total adult population of 35, has a high proportion of low-income residents – mostly students. In 1996, 48% had an income below US$ 20,000 per annum11 In almost all other cohousing communities, attics or basements are rented out. Although renters usually have reduced voting rights, in every other respect they report feeling fully integrated into community life, and feel no less a sense of belonging to the group.

Notes:

1. *The New Shorter Oxford English Dictionary* (1993).

2. *The New Shorter Oxford English Dictionary* (1993).

3. Mandel, D. L. (1996). *Southside Park Cohousing: Program Narrative*. Sacramento: 2.

4. Mandel, D. L. (1996: 2).

5. From the community's guide for new residents and visitors, *Life at The Commons, It's Uncommonly Good: A Guide to Living at the Commons on the Alameda.*

6. Bellah, R. N., R. Madsen, et al. *Habits of the Heart* (1996:116).

7. Kanter, R. (1972). *Commitment and Community: Communes and Utopias in Social Perspective.* Cambridge, Harvard University Press: 225.

8. Marian and Joanne (1996). 'We're Different, We're the Same'. Nyland News: *The Call for Whatever* (October 1996):13.

9. For a fuller analysis, see Hanson, C. (1996). *The Cohousing Handbook*. Vancouver, Hartley & Marks.

10. Reuer, J. P. (1995). *Strategies for Reducing Costs in the Development of Cohousing in the United States and Canada*, McGill University.

11. Meltzer, G. (2000). *Cohousing: Toward Social and Environmental Sustainability*. Department of Architecture. Brisbane, The University of Queensland.

Graham Meltzer
is now a resident at Findhorn in Scotland

Springhill: main pedestrianised street

Pioneering New Build: Springhill

MAX COMFORT

When you see a fully-realised new-build cohousing project which sits beautifully in its urban environment, the mind boggles at the work involved in getting there. Here Max uses broad brush strokes to illustrate how it was done at Springhill.

S pringhill cohousing in Stroud, Gloucestershire, is currently the only new-build cohousing project in the UK based on the original Danish principles. It was the brainchild of David Michael, whose offer for the site – two acres on a south-slope and within five minutes walk of the High Street – was accepted in the summer of 2000. He then went about gathering a group around him who all became Directors and shareholders in the limited company that was to own the site. By September that year, when Contracts were exchanged, some 15 households had signed up, each paying £5,000 for 5,000 £1 shares.

At this point, architects Architype were engaged to work with the group in laying out the site and designing the homes: three-, four- and five-bedroom houses and one- and two-bedroom flats. During this process it was decided to add 12 studio units to the mix. Once the site layout was agreed – positioning the Common House in relation to everything else was crucial – everyone chose their plot on a 'first come first served' basis and paid their plot fee. In the case of the five-bed houses this was £36,000, for one-bedroom flats it came to £18,000. The money thus raised paid back David's deposit of £150,000 and completed the purchase of the site (£550,000) as well as establishing a fund to cover professional fees and admin costs.

While more households joined the group over the winter of 2000-2001 (28 by end of March) a planning application was submitted to Stroud District Council. It had the full support of Stroud Town Council and the Chamber of Trade, who saw this as another feather in the town's cap. However, although the planning officers

External view of apartment block

recommended approval, a group of Councillors decided to oppose the application on the grounds that we 'were going to eat together, would be bulk purchasing and dragging our furniture across the park at night'! The application was thrown out and the officers then had the task of dreaming up 'genuine' reasons for refusal. The group appealed and simultaneously re-applied and in September 2001 we had our permission.

Meanwhile we worked closely with Architype in designing each individual house and flat type. Once a generic design had been agreed, individual households were able to customise their homes, resulting in big variations in layout and accommodation in all the homes.

At the same time we realised that we couldn't get 'self-build' type mortgages on leasehold homes (ours were all to be on 999 year leases, with each household having a share and being a Director of the freehold-owning company, a legal device that is well tried and tested), so David began negotiations with Triodos Bank for a commercial loan to cover the build cost – estimated then at £3.4M on the basis of £70/ft². Despite their excellent reputation, we found the Triodos negotiations cumbersome and eventually turned to the Co-op Bank, who could not have been more helpful. A facility was agreed and once we drew down the first monies, we all started sharing the interest payments – those who were to be living in the biggest homes paid the most interest – around £300/month.

Finding a contractor was a challenge. What we hadn't realised, and were not told by our cost consultants, was that the housing market was overheated and builders were really only interested in nice flat sites, traditional noddy-box houses and a conventional developer client (ex-accountants in smart suits!). Naturally, a difficult site with unconventional homes (we were probably

External view of common house and drainage 'swale'

Dining area, common house

the first triple-glazed housing development in Gloucestershire) and a 'dead weirdy'* client, was not very attractive to contractors intent on making as much hay as they could while the boom still shone. We went through partnering, design-build and, after a frustrating year during which we almost gave up (silly quotes of £6.7M and £7.2M from two builders) we settled on a Management contract (cost-plus) with a local builder, John Hodson. The contract suffered delays and significant price hikes (from our somewhat naïve £70/ft² to £120/ft²) but, eventually, in September 2003, the first phase of cohousers moved in; by the Spring of 2005, the project was complete, with the Common House built last, contrary to our original intentions. Final build cost was around £4.2M.

Now, three years on, it all seems very normal to us but we have regular – and increasing – groups of visitors on our open days, most intent on replicating what we have achieved.

A few stats:

- 34 units on two acres; 6x five-bed houses, 6x four-bed houses, 8x three-bed houses, 4x two-bed flats, 4x one-bed flats and 12 studio units, some of which have been amalgamated to form maisonettes.

- 75 people approximately, including 25 children, ranging in age from 3 days to late 70s.

- A mix of single men and women, couples without children, single parent families and families with up to four children.

- One dog and 14 cats (seven per acre quota)

- Parking is to one side of the site (one per household in our planning approval) with the rest of the site fully pedestrianised.

- All houses and flats are timber frame with 150mm Warmcell insulation, and triple glazed. All houses have photovoltaic tiles which were monitored by the DTI, who gave us a £321,000 grant.

- We have SUDS (sustainable urban drainage system) which worked perfectly in the dreadful floods of July 2007.

- We eat together (if we wish) every Wednesday, Thursday and Friday evening, with a 'pot-luck' on Saturday. We all have to cook at least once a month. Meals are vegetarian despite a majority of meat and fish eaters (it's easier that way) and cost us £2.60.

- All homes are completely self-contained and there is no compulsion to 'join in'; however, the Common House is treated as an extension of our living rooms and we have 24/7 access to it.

- We are required to do 20 hours community work a year, consisting of deep-cleaning the Common House, looking after the boundaries, and other maintenance tasks.

- We have a very low turnover (four units in three years), with most movements occurring within the community; only one home made it onto the open market. If we wish to sell, we have to give 28 days notice to the freehold-owning company of our intention to do so at a certain price (which we choose) and they have the right to put forward people from the waiting list to make an offer, which we are not obliged to accept, however.

- When homes change hands, they do so at around 15% to 20% premium over similar properties in Stroud. By being our own developer, we have gained from the notional 20% developer's profit and the value of our homes significantly exceeds the build cost.

Lessons learnt:
- Pick the professional team very carefully: we experienced difficulties in that some of the professionals didn't respect us and this, in our

experience, led to less than full service in some cases.

- Don't beat the professionals down too much on their fees – you need them to be loyal enough to come out at weekends.

- Use an architectural practice to do the design but consider a seasoned surveyor to run the project on site.

- Don't use internal project managers but do use an external one.

- Don't individualise the homes – it's too much for the professionals to cope with and probably puts the price up.

- Get good advice on realistic build costs before you begin detailed planning.

- Spend time on growing the group – it doesn't work to do the build first and tip the people in at the end, despite what the Americans will tell you.

- Get the 'storming' bit of forming, storming and norming over as soon as possible.

- Expect endless meetings and having to make major decisions in a hurry with very little information.

- It needs a strong, bloody-minded and very, very determined individual or small group to get cohousing going in this country, but there are now individuals and companies out there who are experienced in cohousing and are supporting would-be cohousers, working closely with developers, local authorities, carefully selected professionals and land-owners.

* Quoted from one of the opposing District Councillors

Article written December 2008

(All photos in this chapter courtesy Martin Field)

Max Comfort
was one of Springhill's founding members, and now lives at Whiteway

Living with Communal Decision-Making: Laughton Lodge

MEL NOCK

So, the heady days of development are over, you've moved in – and now begins the rest of your lives. Mel looks at the practical organisation of inclusive decision-making.

Decisions, decisions – How much should the service charge be? Where should we put the trampoline/veg plot/toddlers' sandpit/ornamental pond? Should we revamp the way we charge for heating? Shall we introduce a rota for locking up the common house? My neighbour has erected a washing line which blocks my light – what can I do? Shall we agree to appear in this TV documentary? Must we stick with an ethical bank despite poor customer service and worse interest rates? Do we want this free minibus/swimming pool/stage – but we have to take it this week? Can the village toddler group use our hall for free? How much shall we spend on a summer party? Can I have a rabbit/chickens/sheep/camel? My child wants to celebrate their fifteenth birthday with 50 friends and a light show...

These decisions are much more difficult than those made by other organisations or by families. They affect people's disposable incomes, they impact on their personal, perhaps much cherished vision for the community, they may determine some aspect of their personal lives and personal autonomy, they may challenge their values. And the outcomes are there all day, every day – people do not "escape" them when they come "home".

In the early days of a new community, decision-making will be more intense and more stressful. There are more decisions to be made as the infrastructure is established or implemented. Community members may have less experience of consensual decision-making and may be more worried about loss of personal autonomy. Over time, communities tend to relax as members come to realise that few decisions are as drastic as they may have thought.

View across grounds

Consensus decision-making

It is because these decisions are so embedded in the fabric of peoples' lives that consensus decision-making is so important. A contentious decision made by majority vote will forever remind the minority that they were not heard or not valued. It will forever serve as a little alienation. Majority voting – even occasionally – also opens the way to a much more political environment and to the potential for cliques and factions and for powerful individuals to take more control.

At the same time, sitting in the third meeting on some difficult subject, trying to find an acceptable way through apparently irreconcilable positions saps energy, patience and goodwill. If disproportionate concessions are made to individuals simply to get a decision made, the long term impact on the health of the community may be as bad as a majority vote.

Decision-making made less painful

Here is a guide to some tools and approaches which may help to take the heat out of the decision-making process.

1. Have a clear process for major decisions and be rigorous about using it

Wherever possible, proposals and issues for decision should come from a small group rather than an individual. This might be a standing sub-committee of some kind (the finance group, the common house group etc) or it might be a small group convened specifically to address the issue in question. Initial scrutiny by a sub group will help identify potential areas of conflict and aspects of the decision which will need more information gathering or clearer explanation.

Where the decision is recognised as being potentially difficult or important – perhaps because it has serious financial consequences or sets some kind of principle or restricts residents' freedoms in some way – it can be very valuable to schedule an initial discussion without any intention to make a decision. This frees members from the stress of reaching a decision and allows for a much more open discussion of the reasons for the decision, the potential options and their implications and of any 'concerns'. It identifies where more work may need to be done and may also produce new approaches to dealing with the issue.

When the issue returns for a decision, it must be very clear what decision the meeting is being asked to make. Are they asked to endorse a specific proposal? Or to choose from a range of options? Or to agree a principle which will then be worked up into a more specific action plan? It can be helpful to have an individual or small group responsible for setting meeting agendas whose role will include ensuring that there is a clear question put to the meeting.

It is very helpful if information is circulated in advance of the meeting giving the background to the decision and the reason for seeking it. Then support is provided to ensure that everyone is able to participate in the decision-making process on an informed basis. An authoritative presentation of this information at the meeting builds confidence.

And finally, ensure accurate, sufficiently detailed minutes are kept which will allow anyone not present (or later anyone who has forgotten) to understand exactly what was agreed. 'The proposal was agreed' will come back to haunt you! 'It was agreed to site the trampoline by the back door of the common house, ensuring sufficient space for pushchairs to pass between the door and the trampoline – see attached plan – and to review the decision in a year's time' is much better.

Make a conscious decision about whether to make the decision subject to review – some decisions should be evaluated to check that they have had the intended effect, others might benefit from a regular review to check that they are still right for the community – eg membership of some other organisation.

2. Introduce some policies
Where repeated decisions have to be made, a policy framework can simplify the process. Policies for issues such as external changes to houses including extensions, private use of outdoor space, parties (private and communal) can set out the principles governing decisions. If agreed principles are in place and are clearly followed, it may then be possible to delegate decisions on these matters in some cases at least to a sub-committee of some kind.

3. Delegated responsibilities
Have a clear system of delegated responsibility to sub groups/work groups. Its worth spending some time getting this right – it can save a lot of time and energy in the long run. If the community as a whole agree terms of reference for any sub groups or similar groups, together with a framework for delegated decisions, those groups can be empowered to take on significant amounts of community work in an efficient way. Typical terms of delegation might be to allow spends against agreed budgets and in line with agreed workplans up to the limit of the budget and/or up to a ceiling on any single spend without further reference to the community. Circulating copies of all minutes ensures transparency and sound financial procedures ensure probity without the need for everyone agreeing every decision.

4. Know your own supporting documents
Typically the most contentious decisions occur over a) significant financial decisions – raising money as much as spending it and b) the boundary (physical and principled) between the private and

public – the limits of individual autonomy and collective responsibility. The lease and, to some extent, the constitution, provide the framework for some of this. A sound understanding of what is covered by the lease and what would require a lease change to enact can prevent confusion and muddled decisions which are challenged later.

Allied to this is a clear understanding of whether the community has any underpinning principles which everyone accepts on joining the community. Make a clear distinction between these – which should be few enough and strong enough to be reviewed very rarely – and other decisions shaped by factors which went beyond the pragmatic but which can be reviewed in the same way as other decisions.

5. Good records
Allied to a good knowledge of your own legal framework is a good knowledge of and good records to support your own history. Being able to remember or look up previous decisions which have been made and understanding why those decisions were taken can be very helpful in preventing too much revisiting of issues. Of course times change and new people bring new perspectives but if original decisions were well made, the chances are that they will hold.

Converted "villas"

6. Good information

If the community keeps good information about its activities – how much it uses of key resources, how much it spends on key activities, how often it does things, how many people take part in key activities, how often certain things happen – it will be in a stronger position to take decisions based on an objective evaluation of the facts. Although this does not necessarily make decisions any easier to take, it can make them less contentious. If the facts speak for themselves, more energy can be directed to finding solutions to the problem.

Tools and approaches for meetings

There are many ways of running effective meetings. However, here are some tools and techniques which have worked for some communities.

a) Meeting roles

Almost all meetings work better if effectively chaired. It can be a useful investment to develop and train a small group of people who regularly serve as chair and who have the respect and confidence of the rest of the community for their capacity to be fair and to keep control of the meeting and its agenda. There can also be room for other roles in support of the chair;

- Time keeper – to ensure that the meeting is aware of its own time allocations and consciously chooses whether or not to over run.

- A process facilitator – functions can vary but they can include ensuring that agreed processes are adhered to, checking that everyone feels able to contribute if they want to, watching out for issues left unresolved.

- Minute taker – technology now allows for easier contemporaneous minute taking – it can be a very effective tool for checking that consensus has genuinely been achieved for the minute taker to read out the text of any agreed decisions.

b) Discussion

Where contentious or very significant issues are to be discussed, the meeting might experiment with:

- Round table statements – where the chair goes round the table inviting all members to give an initial view of the issue or to set out any specific concerns or points they have. This exercise can be repeated during the course of the discussion to check on progress.

- Small group discussion. Particularly useful for a preliminary discussion – the meeting can be split into small groups and asked to identify the key issues which will need resolving around a more substantial matter. This is a good way of ensuring that everyone participates or for situations where potentially unpopular points of view need to be put on the table. It can also be used for gathering potential options or solutions.

- Sticky dots. A way of testing support for different options – members are given sticky dots to put against options written on flipcharts. This identifies any options with little support to eliminate and those which are worth focusing most of the discussion on – but beware again of using as a proxy for voting and remember that an apparently little supported option may have one or two committed promoters who cannot be sidelined just because of a dots exercise.

c) Testing consensus

The coloured card system – all members are given a set of cards, green, blue, red, yellow – corresponding to: happy with the proposed decision; broadly happy subject to a specific detail; not happy; not totally against but unhappy about a substantive aspect of it. At points in the discussion, they are asked to show the card which corresponds to their position on the issue. This gives the meeting as a whole a visual picture of whether the discussion is advancing or not and whether discussion needs to be focused on specific areas. It is very important not to use it as a proxy for voting.

d) Other

A strict time limit on discussion can be useful for decisions where the community's response is uncertain. If agreement is not reached within the time agreed, further work which may include detailed discussions outside the meeting with specific individuals, takes place before the issue comes back for a further attempt.

When agreement cannot be reached

Consensus decision-making can be frustrating. In situations where a single individual cannot agree to a proposal which everyone else is content with, the impetus to move to a vote can be overwhelming. Until you are that individual.

Inside the common house on a planning day

Stuck decision-making tries the collective patience. Better to see it as an opportunity for everyone.

- Have the dissenting voices been properly heard and understood – can a "friend" have the conversation again to make sure that understanding has taken place? Are we missing something in our impatience? Can the dissenter agree to a compromise of some sort if they feel that their issues have been sympathetically received and their generosity in stepping back acknowledged?

- Has the proposal been properly understood by the dissenters? Can they be given more information to give them greater confidence? Do they have fears which need addressing?

- Can we return to first principles – are we completely clear about what we are trying to achieve and why – does the dissenter have a different perspective?

- Does the decision actually need to be implemented in the same way for everyone? Is there something specific about the dissenter's circumstances or needs which we can accommodate without sacrificing the principle? Is this something which can be tested or piloted to help the dissenter assess its merits in practice?

- Can we creatively think of an entirely different way of meeting the objectives we were seeking to achieve? Involving new people may bring a new way of seeing the issue. The dissenter may have solutions to offer – can we slow down enough to give them serious thought?

- Is the issue and the need for a decision so strong that it is worth sacrificing the principle of consensus for?

Evaluation

When the dust has settled after the most difficult decisions, there is much to be learned from a review of what happened and why. Typically, barriers to good decision-making will include:

- Decision too rushed – pressure applied to make a decision but actually the issue is not urgent but important. People need time to understand the issues and think about solutions and they find strong time pressure stressful and confusing resulting in opposition rather than considered criticism.

- Insufficient preparation. Inadequate information to support the decision or poor explanations of it.

- Lack of clarity – meeting confused about what it is being asked to decide and why.

- Wrong level of decision-making – the issue did not require a whole community decision.

- Wrong type of decision – never try to decide the menu or the décor or the play list by consensus. Give the job to an individual you all trust and leave them to get on with it.

- Lack of openness – people came with fixed views and were unwilling to take a more lateral view of possible solutions.

- Personality clashes/power struggles – people were unwilling to participate openly because of the views of someone they had a personal antipathy to.

- Vested interests – people being asked to make decisions in the interests of the group which go strongly against their personal interests.

Training and learning

Successful consensus decision-making does not come naturally – although the skills once acquired will be invaluable in many other situations. In particular, community members need to develop:

- Good communication skills. It is important that people articulate clearly their concerns, their views, their emotional needs around specific issues. It is equally important for individuals and the group to listen.

- Creativity – good consensus based decisions are often highly creative ones, synthesising the needs of a diverse group of individuals to achieve a solution which all can live with. Anything to encourage and promote creative thinking will help.

- Rigorous attention to process – good information, sound proposals, clear objectives, accurate minutes – all have a contribution to make.

- An ability on the part of the individual to understand when to let something go and when to stand firm on an objection.

- Sensitivity in helping people to do the above and respecting them for it.

Examples of consensus decision-making

Here are a couple of real decisions made by Laughton Lodge, which illustrate some of the dynamics which come into play with consensus decision-making.

Easy (ish)

The common house sub-committee felt that the common house needed more care and attention than it was receiving and the guests rooms needed better management. They proposed that a section of the common house should be converted into a studio flat and a resident caretaker appointed. They sought the community's agreement to (a) appointing a caretaker, (b) for a budget for the building works, (c) to the change of use of part of the common house.

There were a number of concerns; these included a) cost effectiveness, b) loss of amenity due to the conversion of some common space into private living space, c) whether this would meet the needs identified.

Following the initial presentation of the proposal at a meeting where these concerns were aired, members of the sub-committee:

- Talked individually to residents about their concerns. Specific efforts were made to deal with the loss of amenity. This included finding another space for some of the activities which had previously gone on in the space now to become the studio flat and making further changes to another space to enable it to be more suitable for a range of uses

- Showed how their proposal would generate revenue through the caretaker paying some rent – and how long it would take to recoup the money spent on the conversion

Additional common building and boiler house

- Produced a list of tasks which the caretaker would be expected to carry out

- Invited the potential caretaker to a meeting to talk about his views on his role.

The community agreed the proposal subject to a review in a year's time.

Although this proposal involved significant expenditure, substantive change in the way spaces were used and a new way of working, it was relatively straightforward because the proposers

- were clear about the problem to be addressed and the way in which their solution would address it

- were able to show an overall positive financial benefit

- worked with individuals to resolve their issues outside the meeting – and were open to further change as a way of meeting those minority needs

- put a time limit on the trial period – and actually produced a review which involved everyone – at the end of that period.

Converted 'villa' accommodation

Hard

The community had a shared heating system. For some years, members had been charged for their heat according to a particular formula. The sub group responsible for the heating system had come to the view that this was an unfair system. They had arranged for a new type of meter to be installed in each house and for the data from those meters to be the basis of a new system of charging. Because of the way in which the community's accounts worked, the new system would be applied to the previous winter's heat.

The proposed new system was presented to a main meeting and discussed at some length. The majority of residents agreed with the proposals or were indifferent to them. A small minority were bitterly opposed and would not agree to them. After the first meeting, discussion continued on email and individually but the minority could still not be satisfied. The issue returned to another meeting – still without resolution. At this point, other members became dissatisfied and suggested that further discussion was fruitless and that the voting procedure should be invoked. The focus of discussion then switched to the question of whether and how the voting system should/could be used. Eventually, the minority agreed to stand back and the proposal for a new charging system was agreed by consensus.

This decision was difficult because:

- the new charging system had "winners" and "losers" – but the proposers felt that the actual differences were not that great and were not greatly moved by the objections from some of the "losers". Some of the proposers were "losers" themselves.

- the system was being introduced retrospectively and some of the objectors felt this took away personal control over the size of their heating bills. They felt that had they known about the new system before it was introduced they might have heated their homes differently. The proposers felt that delaying the introduction by another year could not be justified in the overall best interests of the community.

- the proposal involved complex technical and mathematical considerations and formulae. Many members of the community were not able to engage with the detail of these and made their decision on whether or not they "trusted" the judgement of the proposers. When the objectors queried the detail, they became bored and impatient.

- the objectors focused primarily on their own interests and needs – which they felt were being sacrificed to the needs of the majority. The proposers were impatient at the objectors' apparent reluctance to see the proposal in the round.

- the proposal touched on issues of personal values, personal finances and lifestyle choices.

- the proposal had taken a long time and lots of detailed work to develop – the proposers felt they had done this work in good faith and in the best interests of the community. They felt their work was not valued by the objectors.

Ultimately many residents were deeply unsettled at the idea of voting and more people engaged with the process of finding a way to enable the objectors to accept the proposal. The circumstances of one of the objectors changed. Work was done to ensure that residents had much more access to information about their heating costs as the next winter progressed (rather than being presented with a bill sometime in the spring) and work was also done to improve the efficiency and lower the costs of the system overall.

(All photos in this chapter courtesy Martin Field)

Mel
is a founding resident of the Community Project (Laughton Lodge) in Lewes

Models from Mud: Threshold Centre

ALAN HEEKS AND
CHARLES COUZENS

The authors explore some of the unmet needs in the UK affordable housing market, how community housing partnerships could help to meet these, and give specific suggestions on how to make this model more easily reproducible.

We know pretty well what to do about technological sustainability: biomass, super-insulation, passive solar, wind energy and other methods to cut heating and electrical energy use to a fraction of current levels. The new frontier, the much tougher challenge, is lifestyle sustainability. How do we persuade millions of people to change their travel patterns dramatically, halt the ballooning use of private cars and air travel for work, social and leisure travel? Similarly, how do we create a major shift in food habits, back to locally grown, unpackaged, seasonal food with minimal food miles? The radical response to these issues is land-based subsistence communities like Tinker's Bubble or Brithdir Mawr. It's really encouraging to see national papers featuring these projects. They help to sound the wake-up call, but we know most people couldn't conceive of living in this way. The importance of eco-villages and cohousing is that they offer forms of lifestyle sustainability that mainstream society can relate to, learn from, and apply.

It is extraordinary that most attention from government and others regarding energy saving focuses on emissions for home heating. If every UK home was zero-carbon, this removes less than 20% of typical domestic energy use: the biggest uses are food and travel. The reason these are so hard to tackle is that sizable savings depend on sharing resources between households, which is really hard in our housing system. Cohousing can make easy the changes in lifestyle needed to cut these energy uses. Many cohousing schemes already have pool cars, ride-sharing, community food growing, and reduce the need to travel by having work and social facilities on site.

The original farmhouse, now the Threshold common house

Unmet UK housing needs

Whilst community land trusts (CLTs), cohousing and other recent initiatives can pioneer much greater sustainability, the number of new projects reaching fruition is painfully low, highlighting the need for new delivery mechanisms to speed up progress. It is clear that the aims and skill set of most private developers makes them unable to meet these needs. Even approaches by the cohousing and CLT movement towards progressive eco-developers have met with only limited success. During the UK visit of McCamant and Durrett to the Cohousing Conference in 2010, reviewing the relevance of their successful US cohousing model to the UK, it was clear that mixed-tenure cohousing is a scenario for which their model has only partial answers. This is an essential challenge to overcome in the UK: to meet demand, and because of its wider social benefits, to ensure that cohousing does not become an elite form of housing provision.

Other needs which are not being met by current housing delivery mechanisms include:

- A rapidly growing percentage of UK households that are made up of single parent families, single people and older people, many of whom want more social and practical support, and more sense of a safe neighbourhood, than they can currently get.

- Achieving current UK pledges for carbon emission cuts will need dramatic cuts in domestic fossil fuel use: the key to this is sharing resources between households, eg biomass district heating systems, community market gardens, car pooling, ride sharing etc. Food and transport are the largest elements in average household energy use.

- A continuing urgent need to increase new affordable housing provision, and to reduce the dependence on conventional private developers to provide much of this.

The benefits of more new-build community housing schemes run far beyond the immediate occupants: role models are still needed for new local approaches to sustainability and affordability, and can also act as the catalyst to create facilities for the whole population, eg car clubs, alternative energy schemes, and market gardens.

A low-income group whose needs are particularly badly served is the intermediate affordable housing category: this is people who are typically in work or retired, but on low incomes, and who are not prioritised for social housing provision or for grant support by a housing association or the Homes and Communities Agency (HCA). They have limited money of their own to put into the development of a new scheme.

The Threshold Centre:
Piloting mixed-tenure cohousing
Most UK cohousing schemes rely heavily on funding from middle class households with capital, and do not address the needs of low income groups. The Threshold Centre in Dorset is significant in being the first mixed-tenure cohousing scheme to have been built in the UK, and the first to involve direct partnership with a housing association.

This project evolved from a larger project, initiated by Alan Heeks in 2002, which aimed to create a cohousing ecovillage in Dorset. In late 2004, Alan and a few other potential residents agreed to create a pilot cohousing scheme and education centre aiming to get started as soon as possible. They noted that many cohousing groups had been seeking sites for several years without success, and adopted a different strategy: to buy an existing property which could be occupied on a pilot basis and converted to create a cohousing community. By November 2005, six individuals had formed a non-profit company and bought Cole Street Farm, just outside Gillingham in North Dorset. The property included a large stone farmhouse, seven holiday cottages, and two large barns suitable for conversion.

District Council planning policies required 30% social housing provision for schemes over ten units. Initially, the Threshold Residents Group assumed that this project would not be of interest to a housing association, due to its unusual nature and small size. The original planning application in late 2006 was for a total of 11 units, including change of use for the seven holiday cottages, and with four units being low cost market housing whereby affordable purchase prices would be subsidised by the owner-occupiers. In 2007, this application was narrowly rejected by the local Planning Committee: key reasons were the view that the level and quality of social housing provision was not enough to justify the exception needed to local planning policies, that it would be better to have a housing association involved, and doubts as to whether cohousing would appeal to people on the local Housing Register.

At this stage, the Residents Group approached three of the designated housing associations for the District. Of these, only Synergy Housing Group showed both real enthusiasm and understanding of the innovative benefits of cohousing. A Synergy project manager was fully involved with the owner-occupiers in working with the architect, preferred contractor and other professionals in creating a revised scheme for the site, with 14 units, 50% being affordable rent or shared-ownership. Given the many challenges of converting old farm buildings to high-level sustainability within tight cost budgets, input from Synergy throughout this process was crucial, as was joint funding of the professional fees.

The revised scheme was unanimously approved by the North Dorset Planning Committee in November

2007. One of several vital factors in achieving approval was research jointly undertaken by Threshold and Synergy to assess levels of interest in cohousing at Threshold from people on the local Housing Register. A mailshot was produced jointly by Threshold and Synergy, and was then mailed by the District Council to all the 500+ contacts on the local Housing Register explaining what cohousing is, the intended scheme near Gillingham, the special benefits and obligations of cohousing, with an invitation to an open afternoon at Threshold. Over 50 households responded to the mailshot, over 30 attended the open afternoon, and 24 households registered a strong interest in living there.

Threshold accommodation units

Threshold accommodation units

A crucial principle, which was emphasised and checked at all meetings with the District Council, was the 'double-hurdle' approach to selecting residents for the social housing. This means that all social housing residents must be screened not only through the criteria of the local Housing Register, but then through the criteria of the cohousing community. This principle was fully accepted in all discussions. The reasons for this second screening include the need, as in most cohousing communities, to have diversity of age, gender and skills in order to be viable, also the obligations required of all residents regardless of tenure, would not be acceptable to some people. Threshold had already established a selection process for owner-occupiers, and Synergy asked that exactly the same process should be applied to their households, both rental and shared ownership. This process requires potential residents to spend two weekends or equivalent staying at Cole Street Farm. New resident criteria include balancing the overall mix of the whole residents group with regard to age, family type, skills mix etc.

As usual in cohousing, a non-profit company owns the freehold of the site and shared facilities, and sells leases on the residential units. At Threshold, owner-occupiers buy a lease for 95% ownership of their unit, and a single head lease was used to sell the seven rental and shared-ownership units to Synergy. All of these leases embody the same resident commitments. The ownership body is a Community Interest Company (CIC). Normally, the shareholders in a cohousing ownership company are the residents. A new structure was evolved at Threshold to reflect the mixed tenure. Each owner-occupier and shared-ownership household must become a shareholder and has one vote. Synergy owns one share for each of the rental units, but allows proxy voting rights to the tenant in respect of operational matters: the CIC constitution specifies reserved items eg borrowing limits, on which Synergy must be consulted.

Synergy's overall satisfaction at being involved with the first UK mixed-tenure cohousing scheme is evidenced by the commitment already made to work with another, larger cohousing scheme now in the formative stages, in Bridport, West Dorset. Much has been learned by the Synergy team from the Threshold project, which will make future schemes easier to achieve.

The key reasons why Synergy chose to get involved were:

- Innovative form of affordable housing

- Supportive neighbourhood

- Improving affordability through sharing resources (capital and living)

- More sustainable

- Integration with local community

- Less demand on Synergy resources post-occupation.

Some of the key areas in which new approaches, persistence and adaptability were necessary were:

- Overcoming scepticism within Synergy organisation.

- Need to modify Scheme Development Standards, and vary from other guidelines.

- Creating a different form of tenancy agreement, sharing maintenance liabilities between Synergy and residents' management company.

- Negotiating with HCA to overcome their doubts and achieve high levels of grant funding.

- Innovative approaches to meet high professional and build costs of the scheme.

- Creating joint marketing and resident liaison with Threshold team, and working with their allocations policy.

- Creating a new model of governance and ownership company constitution.

- Finding appropriate contractual forms for the build programme.

- How development partnering helps community housing.

The UK Cohousing Network has been researching the faster growth of cohousing in other countries, to understand how to speed progress in the UK. One major conclusion is the benefit of having a developer partner, ie an organisation which already has the skills, credibility and at least some of the funding to make a project happen. The US Cohousing Network identifies this as a key factor in the rapid growth of this sector in North America. The alternative to this is resident-led schemes, ie the residents have to acquire the skills to act as housing developers, they have to raise all the funding needed, and they have to persuade the planning authority, bank, main contractor and others that they are a credible organisation. Most UK cohousing to date has followed this path: its many drawbacks include the need for a super-human level of effort and skill from the residents, and such schemes require (almost) all residents to have the capital to buy their property.

So can a more inclusive, and more achievable model of cohousing be created for the UK? The Cohousing Network has successfully used the precedent of the Threshold Centre to persuade a number of other housing associations (HAs) to consider cohousing, and several HAs are now working with resident groups around the country.

Some cohousing resident groups are reluctant to work with a housing association, fearing that they will be swamped with bureaucracy and over-ridden by HCA and housing association policies and procedures. The experience at Threshold of working with Synergy Housing Group has overall been very favourable, and its cohousing workshops recommend working with an HA from the early stages of a mixed-tenure project. From the residents' point of view the main benefits and drawbacks have been identified as ...

Benefits:

- Development expertise, eg specifications, project management, contractual terms.

- Contacts and credibility in recruiting contractors and professional advisers, some of whom are wary of 'group clients'.

- Funding during the design and application phase, and access to HCA grant funding.

- Convincing the local planning authority that this is a viable, well-grounded project which would deliver affordable housing.

Threshold accommodation units

Threshold's community garden area

Drawbacks:

- The project was made more complex and expensive by the need to meet or renegotiate numerous policies and procedures from the HCA or the housing association.

- Different attitudes to cost: owner-occupiers keen to reduce capital costs and fees, HA more keen to reduce maintenance costs.

- Different attitudes to risk: owner-occupiers could cut corners on minor issues since they would bear any consequences, HA has to be very risk averse.

Another key: The Community Housing Enabler

However, it is clear from the experience of many forming cohousing and similar groups that even the alliance with a housing association as development partner does not make a project easily achievable. Most resident groups do not have all the skills they need to work with professionals, and many regard housing associations as a complication they cannot cope with. Many HAs as well as other professionals lack the desire and skills to work with resident groups to create housing developments. The writers of this paper believe the key to addressing the needs and issues above is to create *Community Housing Partnership Enablers* (COHOPE). The term Community Housing Partnership (COHOP) is a new one which has been created to describe a number of forms of housing provision, such as cohousing, community land trusts and local development partnerships. A COHOP provides housing and other facilities, where a community of residents is involved in the creation, ownership and operation of the site and shared facilities. It should not simply promote 'affordable' housing in its narrowest sense – for those on the Housing Register – but should also provide for the 'intermediate' market, both purchase and rental. A COHOPE would have the expertise, credibility, and access to funding and partner organisations to create a fast-growing number of community housing partnerships to address the needs of specific localities.

The need for this enabling role is especially high for mixed-tenure community housing groups. One reason why more of the purely owner-occupier cohousing schemes have succeeded is that their potential residents typically have more relevant skills, more experience and confidence in dealing with professionals, and more scope to put in large amounts of unpaid time. There is just as much need for community housing among low-income households, maybe even more, but

Threshold's communal gardening area

mixed-tenure groups can benefit greatly from having a professional enabling function, which should be independent of both the residents and the development partner.

The major functions which a COHOPE would need to perform to enable these local schemes are:

1   *Facilitating Local Resident Groups*: Few people have the skills to form a viable community of potential residents which can take a leading role with partner organisations in creating a community housing scheme. This is clear from the difficulties which many housing CLTs and cohousing groups experience. The rapid growth of community housing in other countries, eg US and Denmark, shows that external training and facilitators who have the skills to support and enable potential resident groups can overcome this problem. The roles which this facilitation would cover include: training in group skills such as consensus decisions, conflict resolution; supporting creating group agreements and legal contracts; enabling the residents to communicate effectively with a developer partner, planning authority, and other professionals.

Threshold's communal gardening area

2   *Assemble Partnership Coalitions*: The
    COHOPE will have the expertise and contacts
    to identify suitable partners to work with
    residents for a specific scheme, and to broker
    a partnership arrangement. Depending on the
    locality, suitable partners could include a local
    development trust, housing association, eco-
    developer, building contractor or others. Few
    of these organisations have the experience
    of negotiating and partnering with resident
    groups, but a COHOPE can draw on the relevant
    precedents which already exist to achieve this.
    The COHOPE's role will include liaising with
    potential professional partners, and training
    them in the skills which they will need, as
    well as creating suitable forms of partnership
    contract.

3   *Delivering Funding Provision*: At present, this is
    a major constraint for many community housing
    initiatives. There are two main aspects:

•   *Pre-development Funding*: This would cover
    professional costs for initial site and scheme
    evaluation, architect's and other fees for a
    planning application, and initial legal fees.
    These fees can be substantial, and beyond
    the capacity of potential residents. A housing
    association partner would expect to pay some of
    these fees, but not all for a mixed-tenure scheme.
    The COHOPE will need to locate sources of
    outright grant funding or 'development grants'
    which are repaid if permission is granted, but
    written off if the application fails. Facilities like
    this are already available to community land
    trusts.

•   *Development Finance*: Whilst some input to
    the costs of site purchase and construction can
    be expected from a housing association partner
    and some potential residents, there is likely to
    be a funding gap, especially since a key group
    whose needs are poorly met is intermediate
    affordable housing, ie those who are not eligible
    for the Housing Register, but have limited funds
    to finance a house purchase. The COHOPE can
    work with development trusts and other local
    community finance schemes, or provide access
    to national funding sources.

4 *Engagement with Local Planning Authorities*:
Many local authorities are wary of resident-led
housing schemes, having had poor experience
with badly organised groups in the past. The
COHOPE can provide credibility and skills
coaching for residents, and work with them in
negotiating with planning authorities. It can
also draw on the limited but useful precedents
for planning treatment of community housing
schemes, and help evolve new frameworks to
make this easier in future.

5 *Skills training/support for professional
team*: One of the major constraints on the
growth of community housing provision is
the lack of professionals with experience of
such approaches as cohousing, community
land trusts, etc.: this problem includes legal,
architectural, planning, and development
professionals, as well as housing associations.
Another role of the COHOPE would be to brief
and train the members of the professional team
on the new skills and approaches needed for this
sector.

Bridport Cohousing is intended as a pilot project
including all the COHOPE elements described above.
There is also experience from other community housing groups in the UK, and the US cohousing sector,
which strongly supports this approach. The writers
of this paper are providing these enabling functions
for Bridport, and are seeking funding to document
and share this expertise more widely. They hope to
provide an ongoing COHOPE function in the South-
West, and to encourage the emergence of regional
enablers across the UK.

*(All photos in this chapter courtesy
Threshold Community)*

Alan Heeks
initiated the Threshold Cohousing Centre project in
Dorset, is a UK Cohousing Network Board member, and
is advising Bridport Cohousing. He can be contacted at
data@workingvision.com

Charles Couzens
works with Ecos Trust and Wessex Community Assets,
contact him at charles@ecostrust.org.uk

Affordable Ownership in a Low Impact Setting: LILAC

LILAC CO-OPERATIVE

LILAC is building the first new-build affordable cohousing in the UK, using innovative building and financing techniques.

The LILAC project in Leeds stands for 'Low Impact Living Affordable Community', and is a member-led, not-for-profit Co-operative Society registered with the Financial Services Authority. It was set up in response to a number of key challenges of our age: the need to protect our resources in the face of climate change and energy scarcities, to respond to the housing crisis by providing permanently affordable housing, and to build beautiful, safe neighbourhoods which maximise social interaction between residents and which increase resident participation.

On 25th May 2011, planning permission was granted to build what will be the first ecological, affordable cohousing community in the UK, a planning application for 12 flats and eight houses on an old school site in Bramley, West Leeds, that had received no objections – something of an achievement in itself! The £3M project involves 20 homes (6 x one-bed, 6 x two-bed, 6 x three-bed, 2 x four-bed) and a common house. With a £410,000 grant from the Department of Energy and Climate Change (DECC) and the Homes and Communities Agency (HCA) under their belt, along with a major Social Enterprise Award, LILAC plan to complete by late summer 2012.

The project is based around three pioneering elements.

Artist's impression of LILAC development © white design

Firstly, it is a pioneer of low impact living, in terms of using high performance building techniques and natural materials to deliver buildings to the highest ecological standards. LILAC has chosen to build the houses using a prefabricated strawbale and engineered timber system called Modcell. Modcell is based around individual panels, and high precision cross-laminated timber is assembled into frames and filled with straw and then finished with a lime render. (In fact it is intended that the panels are to be built in a temporary factory near the construction site, where the future residents can take part in their construction.) This system offers advantages over traditional strawbale building in terms of structural strength, building insurance, ease and speed of construction and getting over the difficult and perceptual barrier that building with straw could be dangerous or outdated.

Modcell has been chosen due to the huge environmental benefits of using natural building materials. As carbon is stored and then locked up in natural materials, a typical strawbale house actually sequesters 50 tonnes of CO_2 over its lifetime. It has also been chosen for the manner in which the high performance of the building fabric will help reduce the overall building and living costs of the project over its lifetime, and go a significant way towards meeting the Code for Sustainable Homes (CSH), level 4 standards (which was a requirement of grant funding) without significant additional infrastructure and investment. It is intended to satisfy the CSH4 standards through meeting the space and water heating needs of the community via a combination of a small solar photovoltaic array and 'Mechanical Ventilation with Heat Recovery' (MVHR) units, along with high-efficiency gas boilers with solar thermal water heating units.

The 'Low Impact' outcome will also be delivered through much more than just this kind of building fabric. LILAC aims to reduce the overall ecological footprint of the neighbourhood through positively changing the way the residents live and interact in the community, for example through sharing resources in the common house and through community agreements which outline the ways in which residents use communal resources and open spaces. It is envisaged that a substantial amount of activity in LILAC will centre around the pooled resources of the common house – a shared laundrette, food store, workshop, dining room and kitchen (in addition to the kitchens in the individual dwellings), as well as a multifunction room for events and the local community.

Secondly, LILAC is pioneering a new housing 'affordability' model in the form of a Mutual Home Ownership Society (MHOS), which is an equity-based leaseholder scheme that guarantees affordability in basic housing costs for its members in perpetuity. The cost of buying the land and building the homes owned by the MHOS and financed by the mortgage is divided into equity shares. Each equity share is owned by a member and financed by the payments members make each month, proposed to be equivalent to 35% of individual household's net income. Members take back some of the equity they have paid when they leave, after deductions for depreciation, maintenance and loan interest. The lease that members have to sign also details various community agreements which cover different aspects of community life such as pets, car use and working at home.

The Society's Treasurer Tash Gordon, explains: 'this mutual model of home ownership ensures permanent affordability for residents. Every household pays 35% of their net income to the Society. Equality is at the heart of our model – you pay the same proportion no matter what your income is. And since you can't buy or sell your house, there is no speculation. They remain permanently affordable for future residents and you get back most of the equity you paid in when you leave'.

Lastly, LILAC is pioneering community living in a modern urban context, using clear cohousing principles of a participatory, member-led process that responds to local needs and the skills of group members and the wider community. The site's layout and design will intentionally foster community interaction, wellbeing, safety, natural surveillance and inter-generational support. There is also a purposeful reduction and separation of car use from the car-free home zone area, with only an average of 0.5 car parking spaces per home being achieved through a mixture of car pooling, sharing and a potential car club.

LILAC is committed to having a wider impact and seeing its model taken up by other groups. Paul Chatterton, LILAC Secretary, said: 'In terms of planning, this is a landmark decision. It shows that forward-thinking Leeds City Council is actively encouraging community-led, affordable ecohouses, and this opens up the way for rolling out similar projects across the city and the country'.

LILAC plans to be on site in October 2011, with the project complete by late summer 2012. In the intervening winter, LILAC intends to have a 'flying factory' where the local community will be invited to help build the Modcell wall panels. For more information see: www.LILAC.coop

**Background principles of the
Mutual Home Ownership Model**
The following description from cds co-operatives (www.cds.coop) explains the MHO model LILAC is working with.

Mutual Home Ownership (MHO) is a new form of tenure that seeks to increase the supply of affordable intermediate market housing without requiring a major increase in capital investment from the government. Unlike other forms of low cost home ownership, it is designed to remain permanently affordable and not move out into the open market.

The key is to make land available, as a sustainable community held asset, for the MHO at nil cost to the mutual home owners who will live in the housing built on the land. The land can come from a variety of sources (eg section 106 affordable housing planning obligations, exception sites, surplus land currently in public ownership, industrial land given change of use consent on condition that it is used for MHO, or the application of creative estate management methods).

In MHO, residents pay for the build costs, but not the land. The land is transferred into the ownership of a body accountable to 'community-control', such as a Community Land Trust (CLT) that holds it in perpetuity for the provision of affordable housing in their community. The CLT is the local accountable custodian of the land asset assuring its continuing use for the purpose intended. As the freeholder/head leaseholder of the land, it has the legal power to ensure that the MHO scheme is operated by members as intended.

MHO is a market-equity form of tenure in which residents have an equity stake in residential property. This is because the research carried out for us by the New Economics Foundation clearly showed that the aspirations of key workers and others with moderate incomes excluded from the housing market was to have an equity stake in the housing market.

The residents interested and eligible for the housing are admitted into membership of a Mutual Home Ownership Society (MHOS), a registered Industrial and Provident Society. This must be a mutual organisation for two reasons. Firstly, only a mutual housing organisation is excluded from statutory tenancy provisions. It is therefore free to create the tenure model that grants residents an equity stake through the terms of a contractual lease. Secondly, because it is a mutual, any payment of equity growth to members when they leave is tax exempt, in the same way that the increase in capital value of a home owner's home is a tax free gain.

The CLT grants the MHOS a lease of the land owned by the CLT at a peppercorn rent. The lease contains obligations to build a specified MHO project. It works with a development partner, an RSL (or private sector developer) which takes the development risk (and potential development construction profit) and agrees to build the housing for an agreed maximum price to specified Egan compliant standards. Finance for development is raised through a standard development period loan.

When the housing is complete the MHOS takes out a long-term 30-year corporate mortgage that finances the project construction and development costs. It is a corporate loan rather than a collection of individual mortgage loans because it will be cheaper to residents, in the long term, and will avoid the arrangement and transaction costs, implicit in individual mortgage loans, that erode the benefit of equity growth in other sub market home ownership products. The loan will be structured to give MHOS members the long-term certainty over interest rate risk that Professor David Miles commends in his report on the UK Mortgage Market.

The value of the portfolio of property owned by the MHO is divided into units of property equity (say, £1,000 units, although they could be smaller) which residents fund through monthly mortgage payments under the terms of a long (99 year) lease. New residents will be required to take up and finance a number of units of equity according to their income and ability to finance them. As their salary increases they can take up more units of equity when they become available for sale.

The lease sets out members' occupancy rights and responsibilities, including resident management responsibilities as in a leasehold management company, and the obligation to pay leasehold service costs. It also sets out their right to an equity payment when they leave. The equity payment is due if the value of the units of equity they have funded has increased during the time they are resident in the housing owned by the MHOS. Monthly charges are geared to be affordable at 35% of net income. In effect, the value of the land at nil cost is distributed according to income/need. It is a subsidy that reduces over time for each member as their income rises and they meet their obligation to finance additional units of equity; an obligation that can be enforced through the terms of the lease. All units of equity must be allocated to and funded by payments from members of the MHOS.

Artist's impression of LILAC development © white design

When a resident leaves they assign their lease (occupancy rights) to a new incoming member who cannot afford to buy a home on the open market and who qualifies for housing (if the land is made available for specific categories of key workers). The outgoing member's units of property equity are sold when they assign their lease. Some go to existing members who can afford to increase their equity stake because their income has risen. The balance goes to the incoming member at a lower affordable net cost. The value of equity assigned is determined by reference to an index that is incorporated into the lease. The index is a combination of a local housing market value index and average earnings. This reduces risk by smoothing the peaks and troughs of the property market and helps to keep the housing affordable. This trading of equity shares ensures that the benefit of the land held outside the market by the CLT and the affordability it creates is recycled from one generation of occupant members to the next.

The outgoing member takes 90% of any increase in the index-linked value of units of property equity they financed while they lived in the mutual; 10% remains in the MHOS to strengthen its finances by creating an asset reserve. The 10% is an acceptable retention of asset growth given that the resident has had the benefit of the scheme. This growing asset reserve will enable the MHOS to drive down borrowing costs by lowering mortgage default risk.

These arrangements create a new way of owning equity in the value of residential property. It is a similar way of holding property equity to the way pension equity is financed and held – specified numbers of market-value units are financed by monthly payments and held in a common trust fund until a specific event in time – in this case not retirement from work but moving out and selling equity units held. Equity growth withdrawn is financed by topping-up the mortgage loan.

MHOS members will also be expected to make a personal financial commitment to the scheme by financing 5% of their equity stake as a cash investment in the Mutual Home Ownership Society. This will act as security against arrears of mortgage/service charge payments. It is planned, over time, to develop savings schemes to enable those interested in MHO to save for this investment.

See:
www.cds.coop/about-us/mutual-home-ownership

Key Development Stages: Forgebank

CHRIS COATES

Lancaster Cohousing key development stages: Dawning, adjourning, informing, swarming, yawning, warning, mourning and transforming ...

Forming, Storming, Norming and Performing[1] always seemed too simplistic a description of the stages of group development to me. Here at Forgebank in Lancaster we have done what some have described as a 'textbook' cohousing development – at least we read all the books we could find and tried to follow their advice, but it still doesn't feel as if it has been a smooth ride or anything like an orderly process. But if you want to know – this is sort of how we did it.

Dawning

Back in 2004 a small group of people looked at collectively buying an old school premises in central Lancaster with the view to dividing it up into apartments and turning the tarmaced playground into a big shared garden. I was invited to look round with my builder's hat on to see if the ideas were at all feasible and happened to say 'Oh so you want to set up a cohousing project' and so a seed was sown. The group was outbid for the school by a developer and the playground remains tarmaced as a carpark.

Cohousing is what I've wanted to do all my life, I just didn't find out until now. I've wanted someone to darn my socks, fix my puncture, help me paint and tell me the best first aid remedy as a swap for me, um ... err ... being a friendly face!?! If I'd only stayed in Cardiff where I grew up I'd have had parents, grandparents, siblings, aunts, old school friends, cousins and half the village to help me get by and learn from – but I didn't.

Mark Westcombe –
Founder member Forgebank

April 2006: in the beginning, there were five

A number of us kept talking about cohousing and started to read the available literature (not much from a UK perspective) and tried to find out how others had done it – or tried to do it. After Mark had failed to get to the Community Project in Lewes for one of their 'Learn about cohousing' weekends – it was cancelled due to lack of interest – he was told that a group in Bristol were organising a conference. Well they were, sort of. They had done what we thought was the hard bit. Getting speakers together. But couldn't get anyone to do the room booking /organising catering etc ... donkey work. So on the basis that it would bring everyone involved in cohousing to us rather than us trying to chase them we volunteered and set up an informal group, Lancaster Cohousing Network, to run it. The conference was a great success from our point of view. We got to pick the brains of people who had done it and perhaps as importantly the brains of those who belonged to groups that had not managed to get anywhere. (Rashly at the end of the conference we offered to organise another one – 'after we have moved in' – So that will be 2013 then?)

Adjourning

I think we imagined that after the conference we would be all fired up and ready to get stuck in, but not only did we suffer a bout of collective post conference exhaustion, we also almost to a man, woman & small child had the same reaction: that it all seemed too much like hard work, and cohousing went on a backburner for six months while we recovered our thoughts and our nerves. Eventually someone, I think it was Mark, said over a pint somewhere, something along the lines of 'Well are we really going to do anything about cohousing, or was it all just a nice idea?' This resulted in five of us starting to meet on a regular basis, every Monday, or was it Tuesdays? I remember now we sort of had to draw straws because we all had something on one night or other. Running, Yoga, meetings ... we agreed to sacrifice one thing and change days every now and again so it didn't always fall on the same person. We quite quickly decided that we wanted to sort out a number of things before we got other people involved. They were:

- That there were actually potential sites in the central Lancaster area – we drew up a long list of 12 sites and a shortlist of six from a combination of looking at plans and our own local knowledge. These ranged from sites that were currently on the market, or that we knew had been in the recent past, parts of bigger development sites, or sites that we knew had 'planning problems' ...

- That there was a financial model that we thought would work and that finance would be available – we basically adopted the 'Stroud model'. We talked to the Co-op Bank and Ecology Building Society about a development loan and mortgage finance.

- That we had an agreed bottom line of non-negotiable policies that the five of us could agree to – and that we would not allow these to be changed until after we had moved in.

We held a number of intensive one-day sessions to thrash these ideas out (I remember a very nice week-end in a cottage in Coniston). We did some analysis of the risks involved (the biggest risk turned out to be that we didn't have enough spare time to do the project – it took an outsider to point this out to us). We registered a legal structure (going for a Company Limited by Guarantee as cheap and simple to register and easily understandable by other professionals; banks, building societies, accountants etc.). Then we cracked the first of a number of bottles of champagne to mark the occasion.

Out of these discussions came a simple vision statement:

> 'Lancaster Cohousing intends to build a community on ecological values and to be at the cutting edge of sustainable design and living. However, we would also like our community to be built on trust, respect, friendship and understanding rather than rules and regulations.'

Informing

We then embarked on what we termed our 'widening out' phase to attract more members. This included setting up a website, producing a very short leaflet that signposted people to the website and publicised a number of public meetings where we explained what cohousing was, outlined the project and tried to get folks to sign up to a basic membership for £30 or for a full membership of the project for which we required a £5000 interest-free loan/deposit.

The £5k figure came from a comment made by the Co-op Bank who said they would lend us money if we had enough people who they were convinced were serious about the project – when we said how could we show that people were serious they said 'well if they had invested £5k of their own money in the scheme that would be serious.' I had thought that this would be a real hurdle to people joining. But as it turned out, while it clearly did restrict membership, there were

This page and opposite, artist's impression of Forgebank (artist: Iris Walters, Eco Arc Architects)

plenty of people who could rustle it up. We even had one person who after only having met us half an hour before and seen a quick powerpoint presentation, pulled out their cheque book and offered us £5k there and then. I guess it did make us look 'serious' and one bonus was that for a good while we were able to pay for the expenses of running the group; booking rooms, childcare, etc.. out of the interest on the £5ks that we had sitting in the bank.

We developed a pattern of regular meetings – the Project Development Team (PDT) – the original five of us meeting weekly to do ongoing management of the project, and monthly General Meetings (GMs) of the full membership to keep people up to speed with what was happening and to formulate policies and work on design of houses and site layouts. These also acted as recruitment opportunities for new people to come and find out about us. Often these were full weekend, Saturday and Sunday, events. Both in order to get through the amount of work involved and in order to make it worthwhile for people who were coming from out of town; we have had members from Aldershot, Aberystwyth, Oxford, Aberdeen, Leicester and numerous places in between.

Swarming
Growing from a small tight group of five people who knew each other fairly well to a wider group of 15, 20, 30, ... presented a number of challenges. Some of

them structural – simply needing to have processes and people in place to deal with inquiries, collecting money, booking rooms, chairing meetings. As we grew it became clear that the dynamics of a group of 20 trying to discuss things was very different from a nice cosy group of five, let alone the 50-plus people we could be when we finally move in. Again, simple things like having meeting techniques that allowed enough engagement from members, but didn't end up with meetings of epic proportions. We have done a couple of consensus decision-making training workshops as a group using resources offered by activist networks such as Seeds for Change (www.seedsforchange.org. uk). This has resulted in us using a range of hand signals during meetings and after a while fumbling around for a way to organise meetings, the setting up of a small Process Team who plan and facilitate our main meetings.

We've made some mistakes in the past (and I'm sure will again), but over the years I think we've got better and better at our consensus decision-making process. The harder the issue, the more it has helped us build community. At its best, it evokes brilliantly creative ideas from the group, as we share responsibility for framing and re-framing proposals to be more inclusive. It's awe-inspiring to see our attachment to particular outcomes soften as we work to find a way forward on really divisive issues. At the end the feeling of achievement is tangible. The group is very definitely greater than the sum of its parts!

Diana Martin –
Process Team member Forgebank

We have also instigated workteams around different topics and an expectation that all full members will put in 2-3 hours voluntary work each week towards the project. This was in order to try and spread the load of the work over a wider number of people and to encourage people to be active in the project. This took some time to get working and to realise and cope with the fact that people's abilities and availability vary enormously at times and we had to cope with both the irritation of feeling that some people weren't 'doing their bit' and the guilt of feeling that 'you weren't doing your bit' – my personal feeling is that this can only work out in an equitable way over time (probably talking years here) and in the meantime we need to be generous with each other.

Drawing a big map of the site, September 2010

Yawning

Oh why does it all take so long? I know it's a cliché but when Sarah from the Community Project said at the conference that if she had known how long it was all going to take she would never have started, I only really half believed her. In 2008, three years, three sites and still no project later, I knew what she meant. I do wonder at times how we kept going. We did occasionally say to ourselves 'Is it all worth the doing? Should we call it a day?' But something kept us going. Partly it was the people we had attracted – some of whom thought we were the group most likely to actually get a scheme together – which was both a real confidence boost and a bit of a challenge. From the start we had set up a sweat equity log where we kept track of the management hours we spent on the project (or at least tried to) with the idea that we would get a 'discount' on our house purchase should we reach that point – otherwise it was all at risk. This did help motivation, but I'm not sure it would have been enough on its own. Also, actually getting a site always seemed tantalisingly just out of reach, which spurred us on to try different approaches. For a while we worked with a sympathetic professional Land Agent. We were concerned that we might look like a bunch of amateurs when it came to negotiating a land purchase and consequently were not being taken seriously. He was prepared to work for a 1% commission on the purchase price of any site that he found that we actually bought. We gained a lot of confidence from working with Nigel and an insight into how the property market works, even if at times our collective culture was at odds with the somewhat more ruthless world of property negotiation. In the end we paid him a nominal sum for his help and went our own way, somewhat wiser about the dark arts of buying and selling chunks of land.

Part of the 'project river' - highlights, lowlights, milestones to date, January 2011

Each site we pursued was different. Our first choice was an old British Waterways canal-side maintenance yard in the centre of Lancaster which had remained undeveloped due to poor vehicle access. We were happy to look at a carfree scheme and got support from the local planning dept for this idea. We even went as far as getting some sketch layout plans drawn up. But dealing with a government quango should come with a warning – even after we had made an offer on the site it seemed impossible to get a straight answer from anyone, or even to find out who it was who had the authority to sell us the land. We got to a point of such frustration we were looking to make a complaint to the Ombudsman about the lack of action, when the site was put into the hands of another developer. We then looked at two other sites, almost in tandem with each other. One a small site owned by a local building firm, again next to the canal, who we talked to about doing a partnership development with, and the other a part of a large property development site of over 300 units, where we would have taken a small part of the site and developed it ourselves. Both these sites fell through when the property market crashed. In autumn '08 we decided to give ourselves another six months to find a site after which we would review things with a view to cutting our losses and winding the project up.

Warning

However hard you try it seems that at some point some topic will rise up and bite your nicely worked out decision-making process and seriously test your group dynamics. Seems there is no way round the storming phase, you have to try and sail through it as best you can. Holding on to consensus turns out to be a pretty good boat for negotiating the various waves of conflict that break over you – enough with the nautical references. We have had a number of pressure points during the project; some of them have been background niggles along the way that at times have reared up into full blown disagreements, others have just jumped out and surprised us. Some have been dealt with in a couple of meetings and, if not actually resolved, we have found a way to move on. Others have taken their toll over time, impacting on the project sometimes in quite significant ways. We had a period when it felt like the PDT was under siege with intense email traffic from members becoming a time consuming burden that seemed to threaten to overwhelm some of us at times. This was what in part led to the setting up of the process team to look at group dynamics in a forum that didn't impact so much on the actual day-to-day delivery of the project. Pressure points have been varied and have included: level of environmental commitment, upside down houses and ley lines!

The greatest risk has always appeared when trust has been lacking, then conflict has arisen and people have been afraid that they will not get what they hope for. Despite that, we have only needed a majority vote on one issue, kitchen cupboard colours! and that decision was specifically chosen so we could practise how majority vote would work. We've never had a veto where someone has blocked a decision, we've always been able to improve the proposals and gain agreement. Even those decisions that seemed very difficult have been achieved through consensus, usually by surprising or unusual solutions being found. Getting to the solutions has certainly been painful at times, it's hard for us all to see that a win-win might be possible, it's irritating to be trying to get one and find others have given up. Mind you in the most recent conflict about whether we could have vaulted ceilings on some of the houses I had reached a contented acceptance that we'd failed to see a solution when people who didn't particularly care about the ceilings managed to drive though the solution that kept everyone happy. That was amazing, it had been very difficult and emotive, it was wonderful to be proved wrong.

Elizabeth Mills –
Member Forgebank

Mourning

Along the way people leave for all sorts of reasons although other groups have said that they were amazed at our low level of turnover. This was certainly true in the early days (years!) but we have had our share of members leave. We had a couple of times when we paused and allowed a chance for people to reflect and opt out of the project; one when the housing market went into freefall and some members' circumstances changed. The other when we actually settled on a site, when it really did start to become real and the location didn't suit some people. Leaving can be difficult for both sides, after five or so years of working with people, sometimes in intense situations and while trying to build/forge community, and the loss can be more significant than it appears at face value. One of the risks we identified was a key member leaving but we didn't really work out what to do or what it would feel like when they did. We have found ways to welcome members into the group, but are not so good at saying goodbye. From the inside, suddenly someone you have learned to work with and rely on for support, ideas, friendship ... is gone and you have to adjust and the needs and wants of the project and the rest of the group crowd in and both help to get over the loss, but also get in the way of really getting some sort of closure – or just finding a way to say thanks to parting members. Of course sometimes there is a sense of relief if the person leaving has been a hassle and it is much harder then, but ought to still be possible somehow, to say thanks for being part of the journey to community. For the person leaving it can be just as hard:

The mourning happened during the period of trying to decide whether to stay or leave. The reality of leaving was like a gradual dawning rather than an indecision. The situation we were in had changed such a lot since the beginning: different job situations, housing markets, different desires, and different potential futures. And so for a while there was the dream and the reality and they ignored each other. I ignored them. There is such a momentum in doing cohousing that it is easy to ignore these things because there is so much to do. Who's got time to think! Cohousing becomes your whole life and so how can you imagine yourself without it? All of these people that you have tangled yourself up with, what will it be like without them? What if the loss is too big? And this imagined future, how to let go of that? Now I am completely immersed in a different set of relationships and the mourning is over. It ended when the ties were completely cut, when the contract ended. And now when I bump into people from Lancaster Cohousing I feel a healthy respect for what they are still doing and a warm connection, as if we used to be neighbours, as if we shared our lives, which I guess we did.

Natalie Gill –
Ex-founder member Forgebank

Transforming

Then when we actually got a site everything changed. Suddenly, what was speculation became a reality in front of you – and a different reality than we had imagined. We had been looking for a site in a location fairly close to the city centre and had been ignoring sites further away. Then the market crashed and we were advised to look for 'distressed sites', that is bits of land where the owner has to sell for some reason. A friend pointed out a site where the developer had gone bankrupt and the site was up for sale through the receiver's agent. Some of us went 'I don't want to live 3 miles out of town!', but slowly as we each went and looked at the site this turned into 'Why was it I didn't want to live here?' and even 'Why would you not want to live here?' And it took some imagination to see the potential in a collection of derelict industrial buildings on a river bank with a whole series of potential risks; flooding, contamination, lack of planning permission, two public footpaths running across the site, having to share the site with a fishing club, local opposition to the previous developer's plans ... The site, however, was potentially available for a very good price and there was the risk of letting it slip through our hands if we focused too much on the risks – and running the risk of never getting a site to build on. Also the site just sells itself the more time you spend down there.

The first time ever I saw the site ... Before I saw the site, the reason I wanted to join Lancaster Cohousing was because I believe in cohousing as a way of life; as soon as I first heard of cohousing, I realised this. But after I saw the site I remembered that long ago, before I ever had thoughts about how people should live together, I was a child who wanted to live in a house in the country with a river at the bottom of the garden. Coming away from the site that day I realised that my decision to follow my principles and become a cohouser meant that I would become a country rather than a city dweller. This was never part of the Lancaster Cohousing vision; if anything, there had been an assumption by the founding members that we would end up somewhere in the city centre. It just so happened that this was the first site we managed to buy. Two years from first seeing the site, in a year's time from now, I will be living in a house in the country with a river at the bottom of the communal garden. I now suspect that this, over any high-minded principles of how one should live one's life, will be the reason why I will daily celebrate my decision to become a member of Lancaster Cohousing.

Miles Doubleday –
New(ish) member Forgebank

We had 15 households on board at the time who were prepared to put in the cash to buy the site and, though it took six months of negotiation, our first offer was accepted and we took possession of the site in a flurry of a different sort of activity than we had been previously used to. We moved into a phase of being landowners with the jobs of sorting out insurance, security and maintenance of the property. Then came the preparation for developing the site: design, planning permission, finding a contractor to realise our dreams.

We took the decision to take on one of our members as a client project manager to run the project from our side – something that someone from Springhill Cohousing had advised against as being fraught with potential problems – but we ignored the advice and have tried to be aware of the difficulties it poses and have benefitted hugely from having a motivated project manager who has risen to the task. (Thank you Jon.) While this was the most active phase of the project so far – it was also the stage where we started to get professional help from outside. We had chosen Eco Arc as our architects pretty early on (2007, I think) and they had helped us out along the way with sketches for sites and generic house plans, while saying 'You don't really want to get us to do any work until you've bought a site.' They now sprang into action and helped us to bring other consultants on board and create a Design Team that would help us through a series of participatory workshops to come up with a site lay-out plan and detailed plans for different house types and the common house. These went through various refinements, costing and cost cutting (sorry, 'value engineering') exercises until we were at a stage to put in a planning application. This took nine months.

Boundary walk, July 2011

Another three months and the planning meeting loomed – we were perhaps in a unique position for a cohousing group in that three members of the planning committee were also members or ex-members of the project. (Lancaster City Council has one of the largest groups of Green Councillors around the country.) This meant on one hand that we were very clued in to local planning policy requirements and local politics, on the other hand it meant we had to all declare an interest and not take part in the actual meeting that decided on our application. As it was we had support from the planning officers and we had done a thorough local consultation with neighbours and the Parish Council which had resulted in there being no opposition or serious objections to our scheme. So apart from one councillor asking if were like the Amish (we are not), another saying we weren't green enough because we were too far away from a bus stop, and someone wondering why there wasn't an angry mob objecting like there had been to the previous developer's proposals, eventually our scheme was passed.

And finally Building

The same month that we were granted planning permission we interviewed potential building contractors who would then work with us and our Design Team on a partnering basis to come up with final detailed designs and costs for the project. Writing this a week before the contractors start on site in the summer of 2011, I think we had all hoped it would have taken less that 12 months to get from planning approval to start on site. But we hadn't reckoned with the complexities of the project and the frustration of dealing with the minutiae of negotiating contracts that needed to be overseen by the banks' solicitors. Only another 12-16 month build period to go and then we can all move in and ... well, start living cohousing.

(All photos courtesy Lancaster Cohousing website: www.lancastercohousing.org.uk)

Note

1. http://en.wikipedia.org/wiki/
    Tuckman%27s_stages_of_group_development

Cohousing: Supportive Local Networks in Old Age

MARIA BRENTON

There is much to learn in the UK from the cohousing communities for older people that have been established abroad.

Although cohousing grew in Denmark as an answer to the needs of young parents and their children, it was soon recognised for its value in maintaining social contacts for people at the end of their lives – that long period after children have grown and moved away. Being able to tap the resources of locality and neighbourhood acquires greater significance through the latter decades of people's lives, as employment roles recede, energy and mobility levels gradually reduce, life becomes more centred in the home and key relationships – spouses, partners or friends – diminish in number through death and divorce. A report on 'The Lonely Society' published by the Mental Health Foundation in 2010[1], notes the decline in recent decades of traditional communities tied to locality and their partial replacement by more fluid 'communities of interest' which tend to transcend local boundaries. With employment still mostly separate from home, the disappearance of local services such as post offices, pubs or the corner shop, a fading affiliation to churches, and the rapid pace of modern life leading to social fragmentation, locals in many areas know each other less well. Neighbourhoods which continue to be 'dormitories' for many of working age may offer little support to those who now, by virtue of their age, find themselves anchored there. Add to this a growing trend towards living alone and there emerges a potential problem of social isolation, often compounded by loneliness[2] among older people.

Single living in old age
In the UK in 2010, 45% of men and women in the 75+ age-group lived alone. Women over 75 are almost

twice as likely to live alone as men, at 60% and 36% respectively. This is part of a general trend. From 1961 to 2010, single households grew from 12% of all households to 29%, evidence of strikingly changed social patterns[3]. DCLG (Department for Communities and Local Government) projections in 2010 forecast a 42% increase in people over 75 years living alone by 2016. This is fuelled by a 31% increase in single living since 2001 among the age-cohort 45-64 years, where single men are a fast growing group. These figures strike warning bells. Living alone and being isolated in old age can have a serious impact on older people's wellbeing which in turn fuels high levels of demand for health and social care services. Having friendly helpful neighbours at hand, finding new opportunities to take part in social activities nearby and discovering fresh ways of making a contribution can make all the difference to personal happiness and health or even survival and are certainly crucial in public expenditure terms.

Castellum, exterior, Amersfoort, the Netherlands

What does cohousing offer older people?
Intentional community development among isolated older people is an investment in ageing well that society neglects at great personal, social and economic cost. A wide body of research on social connectedness attests to the positive impact of close relationships with others on people's health and wellbeing[4]. Studies of

cohousing communities[5] have found that, where older individuals are concerned, the outcomes of living in community can be an enhanced sense of wellbeing, reduction of loneliness and isolation, continued activity and engagement, the possibility of staying healthier for longer and, finally, continued personal autonomy and independence. These derive from:

- A sense of personal efficacy and satisfaction

- A sense of belonging to a community

- Participation in collaborative activities

- Mutual support and security.

The cohousing practices that lead to these benefits include conscious community-building, shared responsibility and commitment, democratic decision-making and continued self-management, shared meals and some involvement in design of the group's environment (the latter for the early residents at least). Senior cohousing groups are also usually based explicitly on mutual support. Beyond the community-building that evolves naturally when getting a project up and running, cohousing usually offers groups opportunities to develop skills through training in group processes, such as conflict resolution, consensus decision-making, facilitating meetings etc. Small committees exist for key functions, like maintenance, gardening, outreach or finance and sometimes for mediating conflict. Working together in these committees or sharing in the management of the whole community is not only a way of building social cohesion but also a way of learning new skills – and learning new skills is a way to keep happy and healthy.

Benefits to the wider society can be:

- Promotion of active, healthy lifestyles

- Reduced or delayed need for health/care services

- Reduction of dependency on the state

- Encouragement of social capital

- Enhancement of civic participation

- Sustainable, green lifestyles

Do older people want cohousing?

A mass of website generated enquiries to the UK Cohousing Network year on year indicates that demand for cohousing does exist among older people.

> We know that cohousing is of mounting interest to older people in Britain from the volume of enquiries we receive from individuals seeking a group to join or advice about forming a group where they can collaborate in an active and companionable old age. And we are aware that the values cohousing stands for – privacy combined with active community and resident control and autonomy – are sought after by a far wider section of the older population than those familiar with the term 'cohousing'.
>
> UK Cohousing Network

Senior cohousing abroad

Cohousing offers two possible models for older people – the first is family-based and intergenerational; the second is the peer-group model, again broadly intergenerational, but restricted to people over 50 or 55 years. In Denmark and the Netherlands both models are widely available. In the United States of America a rapidly burgeoning family-based cohousing movement now has a growing senior dimension, due to the efforts of Charles Durrett. With Katie McCamant, Durrett is responsible for the migration of the cohousing concept to North America from Denmark. His book and his developmental workshops on the subject of senior cohousing are slowly influencing the take-up of cohousing by older people who prefer child-free environments[6].

In the Netherlands, some 200 senior cohousing communities exist, some based solely on purchase, many for social rental and others for mixed tenure. The success of these communities depends on achieving as wide an age-range as possible so that they stay lively. For three decades, it has been Dutch government policy to confront societal ageing by promoting and encouraging the formation of these communities as a means of ageing well and reducing demand on health and social care services. Official recognition of the cohousing concept is widespread and a broad infrastructure of support exists for older people's initiatives in which public authorities, housing associations, developers and small commercial firms all play a part. Public grants are also available for groups to hire the project management skills they need to develop their own small housing schemes. Once up and running,

Nieuw Wede, Amersfoort, the Netherlands: members' flats on left; community room on right

the senior cohousing communities allocate tenancies and manage themselves. In recent years, housing associations have facilitated 'retro-fit' senior cohousing communities – where an apartment block has a high concentration of older residents, for example, those who wish are helped to form an active and mutually supportive cohousing community in situ around the use of a vacant flat used as their common space.

What cohousing exists for older people in the UK?

Apart from the small handful of family-based cohousing communities among which some older residents are to be found, there is, at the time of writing, no cohousing community in the UK for older people who prefer to live in adult-only environments. Despite the long term efforts of a group such as the OWCH (Older Women's Cohousing) Company, London and the UK Cohousing Network to promote the senior cohousing community's benefits as a model for older people, recognition of its value has been slow to grow in the UK. Among other reasons this may be due to:

- Restrictions around land that create scarcity and therefore unaffordability

- A chronic dearth of long-term vision in British social institutions

- Conservatism in the housing sector

- The conceptual dominance of largely outmoded models such as sheltered housing

- A paternalistic approach to 'the old' which sees them only in terms of 'needing care'.

However, there are signs of an encouraging break-through. Wider recognition of cohousing has emerged in recent years from the efforts of the UK Cohousing Network of the need to inform and attract housing associations to the concept. Hanover, in particular, a specialist in providing housing for older people, has adopted a policy of facilitating senior cohousing, giving assistance to OWCH and groups in London and elsewhere. The Vivarium Community in Scotland has been helped by a charitable trust, as has OWCH, to sustain its struggle for a senior cohousing community.

Wendakker, Amersfoort, the Netherlands.

In 2010, Hanover forward-financed the purchase of a North London site for the OWCH group who had been trying to attract the support of a housing association developer for some years for a mixed tenure scheme. By 2013, the group will have moved into a building they helped design, where owners, shared owners and renters will run their own community collaboratively. A small housing association, Housing for Women, a supportive partner through many years, will act as landlord for the rental elements. The major part of OWCH capital financing will come from OWCH members selling up and buying in. In the absence of grants or the support of the local authority, a charitable trust is covering the gap in funding for those without equity. Because OWCH members (aged 55-80 years) could not sustain the risk, Hanover will carry this through to completion. A key condition, for the three parties involved, is that OWCH members remain stable, committed to the scheme and active in recruiting future members.

The sustainability of the OWCH group depends on robust group processes. There is little space here to outline the means by which the OWCH group has maintained its motivation and purpose and how it has built up a sense of community, despite its members being scattered all over London. Suffice it to say, group cohesion and solidarity do not arise by chance. The group has throughout its existence been underpinned by what may be termed a 'project manager' external to but highly involved with the group (the author of this chapter). OWCH members have set up formal structures and procedures, have fund-raised for professional training in many aspects of the group process and have developed an active marketing outreach. They have also given a central place to sociability, to members getting to know each other in small groups and to helping new recruits feel at home.

Senior cohousing as policy

Unless lessons are learned from the experience of the Older Women's Cohousing Community, it will remain unique, rather than fulfilling its wish to be the forerunner of many similar senior developments. This means that those responsible for forming and executing policies to address the inevitable ageing of our society must take their heads out of the sand and do more to assist older people to do things for themselves. More a question of mobilising resources and energies and removing barriers than identifying specific extra public expenditure, it behoves central government departments and local authorities to develop a longer term vision. There should be food for thought and action, at the very least, from a realistic appraisal of:

- The high levels of unmortgaged equity locked up in older people's housing (£1,000 billion in 2006)[7],

- The high concentration of older people in multi-bedroom homes (60% of older households with no dependent children[8])

- The incidence of single living and loneliness among older people (see above).

- Concerns about the mounting and ultimately unaffordable costs of care for the old in the face of societal ageing

The Happi Report[9] in 2010, a government sponsored enquiry into European provision for older people, visited several European senior cohousing communities and, among its key recommendations, urged UK local authorities and housing associations to help and encourage older people to develop these communities. It also urged the promotion of better design to lure the old from under-occupied family housing by offering them significantly more attractive alternative accommodation than has been available hitherto in the UK.

Older people and cohousing
Alongside these imperatives, the re-emergence of mutualism and self-help as politically fashionable ideals should mean that the senior cohousing community moves centre-stage. Its take-up and development equally demands that those who are soon-to-be-old wake up and take responsibility for the societal ageing of which they are part. They need to think ahead, plan and make choices before they reach a stage where they no longer have choice. A future where the welfare state becomes even less a source of the care that ageing and frail people need, depends on the fit and energetic young-old forming local alliances with those who are older in a collaborative setting that encourages activity, involvement and mutual support. That is what senior cohousing is about.

(All photos in this chapter courtesy Maria Brenton)

Ulinthof, Baarm, the Netherlands

Notes
1. Griffiths, J. (2010) 'The Lonely Society', Mental Health Foundation.

2. Allen, Jessica (July 2008) *Older People and Wellbeing.* Institute of Public Policy Research.

3. Beaumont, J. (2011) 'Households and Families' ONS, Social Trends 41.

4. Allen, J. (2008) 'Older People and Wellbeing', Institute of Public Policy Research.

5. Brenton, M (1998) 'We're in charge': cohousing communities of older people in the Netherlands, Policy Press, Bristol; Brenton, M. (2002) 'Choosing and managing your own community in later life' in K. Sumner (ed) Our homes, our lives: choice in later life living arrangements. London, Centre for Policy on Ageing/ Housing Corporation. Fromm, D. & E. de Jong (2009) 'Community and Health: immigrant senior cohousing in the Netherlands', *Communities*, 145, Winter, 50-53; Glass, A. P. (2009) 'Aging in a Community of Mutual Support: The Emergence of an Elder Intentional Cohousing Community

in the United States', Journal of Housing For the Elderly, 23: 4, 283 – 303.

6. Durrett, C. (2009). *The Senior Cohousing Handbook – a community approach to independent living.* New Society Publishers, Canada.

7. Holmans, A. 'Prospects for UK Housing Wealth and Inheritance', Cambridge Centre for Housing and Planning Research, July 2008.

8. Centre for Housing Policy, 2008.

9. Housing our Ageing Population Panel for Innovation (2009) 'Designs for Ageing'.

Maria Brenton
is an independent cohousing consultant who has researched senior cohousing in the Netherlands, Denmark and the USA. She has written and published widely on the subject. She is project manager for the OWCH (Older Women's Cohousing Company – www.owch.org.uk), London and a founder-director of the UK Cohousing Network. She can be contacted at mariabrenton@safeserve.com

Designing for Cohousing

ECO ARC

Andrew Yeats and Lucy Nelson are Eco Arc, the architects for the Lancaster Cohousing project. Here they talk to D&D editor Chris Coates about the project at Forgebank near Lancaster and their thoughts on Cohousing in the UK.

CC Do you think cohousing appeals to a particular generation – that it is somehow a middle-aged thing?

AY Well yes, because you can't join cohousing generally unless you've got some money. Unless you've already had a house ...

LN You've got to be at a time of life where you're looking relatively long-term.

AY You've got to have owned something, or worked pretty hard for a while to have saved up some money to join. So you can't come as a kind of student hippie with lots of ideals and no backing. I think there are lots of reasons why cohousing fails, but getting the right number of people in the right place at the right time with the right assets to make it financially work ... and the right skills ... I think it's virtually impossible – which is why it hasn't happened so much in Britain. There are probably very good reasons why it's happened in Denmark and Norway, but I think they're more socially geared up for it. And financially, the institutions are geared up for it. Whereas over here you've got more to struggle against.

On a day-to-day basis [at Forgebank] we are wrapped up in the minutiae of what we are doing. But when you look at the bigger picture it is absolutely phenomenal that it's got off the ground and got this far and it's now finally happening ...

I also think the other fantastic thing about the Forgebank project is the green, Passiv house aspiration. And I think that ordinarily that would have suffered at the hands of a developer, or individual preferences would have diluted the aspiration and the fact that despite quite tough financial constraints you've stuck to the ideal of achieving Code 6 and Passiv House. In that value engineering process it would have been so easy to throw the baby out with the bath water and say bugger it ...

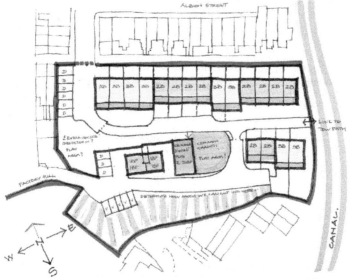

Albion Mills, option A: the illustrations in this chapter are sketch layout plans for early sites considered by Lancaster Cohousing

With much more individualism it would have been harder to achieve an environmental standard like Passiv house or Code 6 and also meet the social criteria and budget. So the fact that you've been able to discipline yourselves has actually made it – not straightforward – but achievable in a way that most projects aren't. And I guess a lot of people come to me starting off wanting some accolade environmental criteria, but as soon as they see the reality of it in their own house they say, 'No, actually I've got a big view to the north I want all my windows facing north'. Then suddenly it's all out of the window. They don't give a toss about anything as long as they can have their view, or they want

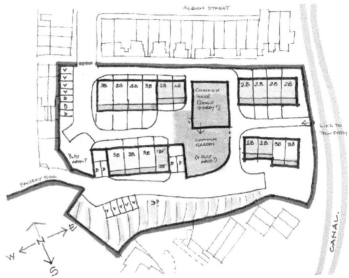

Albion Mills, option B

their open fire because they didn't realise they couldn't have an open fire in a Passiv house.

CC The only time it has been a clear conflict for us has been when the Code for Sustainable Homes doesn't allow for communal solutions ...

AY Just today I had to boycott the Code for Sustainable Homes consultant. He said that to get the tick in the box for the Code, every house has to have three bins outside its front door. I said this is madness. It's going to look like bin alley from beginning to end. It's just mad – we've got bin stores that are nicely recessed in the wall, people will put stuff in there, those bins will then go to a central bin store and that will be fantastic. To put a bin outside every house just to tick a box is mad ...

CC It can't be just Forgebank who are getting communal bin stores. They're going to come across it in other circumstances.

AY What's interesting is that most people have acknowledged that SAP [the government' s Standard Assessment Procedure for energy rating of dwellings] has been fairly useless for ten years and without being unkind I think most people think the Code for Sustainable Homes is fairly rubbish. It's not very flexible and it isn't very negotiable.

CC Interestingly, that's been one of its advantages for us, in that it's something we are aiming to hit – a solid target. Otherwise we could just spend forever trying to make up our own standard.

AY I think it's good to have a benchmark set of criteria. But I also think it's quite difficult when those criteria are not flexible enough to meet your site requirements, or your community requirements. Because it's set up for individual houses, not for community housing. So it's a 'one system must fit all'.

CC How difficult has the common house design been? Because it's a strange hybrid of a building, it seems to me.

AY The common house interior has not been finalised yet – it will have more care and attention lavished on it. Having said that, I remember we had meeting after meeting when all we talked about was the common house. When we issued the contract drawing this week, we noticed that the level of detailing on the houses is phenomenal, in terms of the participation of the structural engineer and Alan the PHPP man [Passiv House Planning Package – a program to assist in design for Passiv houses]. There isn't the squeak of a hint of an air leak anywhere, it's been absolutely buttoned down. But when we got the common house drawing out it was like whoa – we need to work a bit more on this. There's a lot more tightening up on this to do, and that's partly because I've always been nervous that if you make one mistake on one house, or one drawing, it's rolled out 40 times and that keeps me awake at night worrying about it. Whereas with the common house I think well, you know, I can pick that one up and I can fix it and it's just like any other building. It's only one building, and it has suffered a little bit from value engineering. The personalisation and individualisation of the common house has attempted to make it less of an institution and more of a members' comfy cosy place, an extension of the home, but that hasn't quite been achieved yet – some of the detailed interior work needs more work from us and from the group, and of course the choice of furniture and fittings will have a major impact on the feel – there was a bit of divergence of priorities which took some time to resolve and also there were still unknowns around the budget. I think we need to be careful that between now and when we've finished that there is a really active working group that lavishes attention on it.

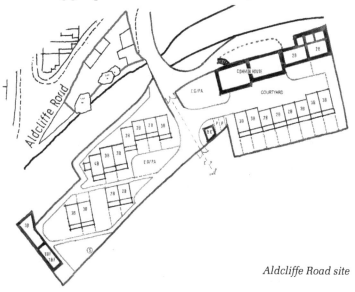

Aldcliffe Road site

What's interesting in setting the context for Lancaster – in a way the pedigree, and the history of where you've come from – is that it's a very respectable, contemporary notion of utopia. It still aspires to utopia, but is a very conditioned, appropriate response to 21st century living. And it's also hugely appealing to a broader spectrum of people who have less radical roots and less radical ideology, but none-the-less still have the nucleus of the impulse to live communally and to share and be part of a greater good that's bigger than the individual. I think that's fantastic. And it also makes it respectable because, without being unkind, if you mention communal living to a lot of people, they would be a bit twitchy about it. But I think cohousing is a reinterpretation at an appropriate level of a fundamentally radical idea ...

CC How crucial is intentional design to cohousing? This is something I keep coming back to. We were down at Postlip Hall, which is one of these Big House communities and they are sort of now calling themselves cohousing. But I would say that they are missing the design element. The house hasn't been intentionally designed for community, and my argument is that you are actually working against the architecture ... So is that design absolutely critical to cohousing? Because I think it is ...

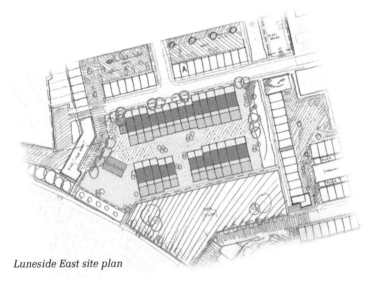

Luneside East site plan

AY I think there is something very magical about the coming together of a group of people to set about a collaborative participatory design process to make something that wasn't there before – rather than just carving something up and sub-dividing it – I think that's something quite different.

LN The probability of it being cohousing is very low, but the possibility does still exist.

AY And there are people who have converted factories and things aren't there.

LN Can you convert an existing building into a cohousing scheme? I'm not convinced that you can. I think one of the outcomes you get from all those decisions you make together is almost like condensing all the interaction that you would have with your neighbours over X number of decades. So I'm not sure that even if you found an existing building that would convert very well, so that you bypass that process, I'm not sure you could build up the trust. When you carve up an existing building, you haven't got the fundamental decisions to make together. So it's as if what you do and the trust you build up gets passed on in a wider community sense to other generations and family and, to some extent, stays with the community. Or does it dissipate when those original individuals leave? I don't think it will dissipate ...

AY In America where they do developer-led cohousing, as good as it is, it leaves me completely cold. And if someone asked me to do that, then I would have to get my head around that. I would have less enthusiasm.

LN It serves a different purpose; it's just different. It's much much easier and lower risk to do it that way, and I can understand why people do it that way. But it is not nearly as pure, and it doesn't have the same amount of creative potential. But it has the potential to produce a lot more homes.

AY And it allows a lot more people to buy in to it without the hassle and ball ache that you've had for the last five years. You can just sign on the dotted line and move in, which must be nice but you must lose something from that. From an architectural point of view for me it is that element of engaged participatory inclusive design that is important. As much as I would like to be a prima-donna designer of utopian communities and people just moved in, that isn't what it's really about is it? It's about you doing it together in some sort of way. Although I have to say I've completely changed my view from when I came into all this lark a long time ago and there was that whole notion of the architect completely stepping back and allowing everybody to design it, and the architect was just a facilitator that then put pen to paper at the end. That completely fell flat on its face at Findhorn, because it became clear – or maybe I was just a bad facilitator! – that people couldn't do it for themselves. That they actually needed somebody, whether it was an architect or someone else to hold it together and then to envision it with them and then put pen to paper. It doesn't happen by itself. And if it's left unmanaged it just becomes anarchistic or it doesn't gel somehow. As architects we try to set aside our own prejudices, but bring some level of experience and knowledge. Somehow we have to let go and imbibe the collective good, of what everybody wants. Then somehow help bring it into reality. But we must take responsibility for it. Because as soon as we let go of the responsibility, somehow it doesn't work. That has been a bit of a sad reality for me, because I came into this project imagining that everybody would do it, and I wouldn't be doing that. Which isn't true really ...

More about Eco Arc can be found at:
www.ecoarc.co.uk/team_yeatsnelson.html

Andrew Yeats and Lucy Nelson

Finding the Right Property and Location

MARTIN FIELD

Martin wades into the Diggers & Dreamers Wiki to pull out an overview of resources.

Finding a suitable property within a budget was, is, and will likely continue to be one of the major stumbling blocks for new intentional communities. There is an inbuilt tension between members until a particular location is settled on, or at least an agreement reached on the area in which the group wish to be located. Should people get together first, and then try and agree where the group wants to be, or do a small number decide on a location and then look for other people who could want to live there as well?

Once that basic issue has been covered, it will not help to be fixated on either a 'countryside' or an 'urban' location – great plots are not always in the most obvious of locations. Recent government directives to make creative use of 'brownfield' sites in urban or rural areas could mean that a place not previously used for residential supply could become a viable location. It might prove a little harder to find something suitable for a cluster of communal buildings, but still well worth investigating as an option.

The UK cohousing neighbourhoods now in existence already demonstrate a large variety in how they acquired their sites. Places like Thundercliffe Grange and Canon Frome were identified by groups looking at the potential for splitting existing buildings into separate units; the initial group behind the Community Project in Lewes (Laughton Lodge) searched through a host of land sale particulars outside of London before coming across the ex-hospital site it acquired in Sussex; the Frankleigh House and Springhill sites were acquired by a single founding member, with the intention of being used as the basis for subsequent group development; the Threshold Centre was a set of farm buildings acquired by its first group of members, who have then needed to find others to occupy the rest of the completed units; and the Lancaster site at Holton (Forgebank) was acquired on the back of the group hearing of previous private sector development plans falling apart, leaving land and ex-mill buildings ready for an imaginative investor.

Although it pays to be imaginative and flexible, if the task seems too far outside the group's immediate skills, it could be advantageous to consider using a land agent to find or negotiate the terms of acquiring a suitable place.

Initial ideas on identifying and appraising potential sites
Current policy proposals from the Coalition Government include the idea that 'asset registers' are created and maintained by local authorities in order to record details of land and sites considered to have some potential for 'community benefit'. This would be for any assets, in any ownership – it is not essential that they are already in some form of statutory or community ownership – only that their potential for community use and gain has been recorded.

If the use of such registers takes off, it would seem to be just the kind of site information that groups would wish to use, along with a kind of practical framework for making a first evaluation of what a site or 'asset' might have to offer. The kinds of issues to include in such a 'potentiality checklist' will be:

- Geographical location of site and character (wilderness, rural, semi-urban, urban)

- Site stability and any potential contamination

- Micro-climate: soil type(s) / drainage / indicative 'water table'

- Existing vegetation and ecological value

- Aesthetics (of the area and any built forms)

- Amount and direction of sunlight (and potential for renewable energy generation)

- Any existing buildings and the scope for their reuse

- Accessibility (on foot, on cycle and by public transport)

- Potential for fit with existing neighbours / neighbourhood

- Prospects for employment / business on or close to the site

- Schools

- Other local and community facilities

- Kinds of site covenants or 'use restrictions'

- Basic acquisition and transaction costs and terms.

Obtaining a site from the public sector

There has been much public debate in recent times on how to make appropriate use of public resources in order to help bring about economic 'recovery'. The government is very mindful of the role that public assets can have in helping new housing and neighbourhood development to happen, especially if sites currently in public ownership mean that some of the excesses of 'private market' costs and demands can be softened, if not avoided all together.

For example, it is no longer the case that public assets must automatically be purchased up-front, and at the highest of 'open market prices', and the government has been encouraging public asset-holders to demonstrate a creative willingness to make acquisition terms attractive enough to encourage hesitant developers to progress with local schemes. One such innovation is an encouragement that public sites are sold/acquired on a 'build now, pay later' basis, where final payment for the site can wait until some future point in time when new properties have been built and sold, providing an operating revenue or sales receipt to be directed back to covering the initial 'purchase'.

Despite calls for there to be a national position set by government for how some of these assets could be deliberately directed towards local 'community-led' ventures, it is being left to local authorities to decide for themselves if there is any need for local policies on how any such asset-release is undertaken in their area. It could therefore become crucial for public sector asset-holders to be lobbied sufficiently hard for them to understand the extent of local demand for 'community-led' ventures, and the evidence that groups and local communities can deliver on such aspirations. If there are land or site resources being offered for development purposes on terms that are designed to help hesitant developments to come forward, 'community-led' initiatives need to register their desire to be treated on equal terms with other more usual partners from the development sector.

Where cohousing and other groups are mindful of the need to lobby their local authority to adopt formal policies that could support land or sites coming forward for 'community-led' development initiatives (even as a part of a 'pay later' site offer to a mainstream developer), the following recent proposals may be useful for suggesting terminology that the authority could use:

All public bodies should be required to publish details of their non-operational land alongside a strategy for its disposal which proactively identifies land with potential community use or benefit ...

There should be publicly accessible asset management registers of all public property, with both mapping information and information about associated operational and policy objectives ...

The presumption that a community group has to make a case to the local authority for acquiring an asset should be matched by a local authority's corresponding duty to make the case for retaining it or selling to another party or for another purpose ...
All from 'Report of the Land & Society Commission', Royal Institute of Chartered Surveyors (2011)

With a view to maximising output ... local authorities should consider the possibility that group self build could deliver a healthy proportion of new housing. Local authorities should be encouraged to make publicly owned land available to an 'enabler' who will control the overall design of the site, divide it into suitable plots and plan necessary infrastructure allowing people building their own homes to develop these plots.
Taken from 'Homebuilding in the UK: a market report', Office of Fair Trading (2008)

... the most innovative and powerful means for local authorities to pursue a sustainable, affordable housing agenda on lean resources would be to 'create' a new class of land specifically designated for self-provision only. This would begin simply by including self-provided housing as a recognised class of development in their Strategic Housing Market Assessments (SHMAs).
Taken from 'A Right to Build', Alastair Parvin, et al, University of Sheffield / Architecture 00 (2011)

Lastly, if a disused property or land is identified by a group that it thinks is owned by a 'public' body – that is a local or county council, health authority, British Waterways, Homes & Community Agency, etc. – but the ownership or future use of the site is not completely clear, information about the status of the site can be found by making a Freedom of Information request. This would be directed at each potential owning body, and could ask such things as – What are the current and future plans for the property? Who is the person who has the lead responsibility for it? When was the last time any work was carried out? Are there any plans to dispose of the property? Under the Freedom of Information Act 2000, anyone may request information from a public authority which has functions in England, Wales and/ or Northern Ireland. (It also applies to the House of Commons, the House of Lords and to the Welsh and Northern Irish assemblies.) The Freedom of Information (Scotland) Act 2002 applies to the Scottish Executive, the Scottish Parliament and the Scottish public authorities. Go to **www.whatdotheyknow.com** – it's the easiest way to make a FOIA request

Obtaining a site through the mainstream development / house-building sector
The corollary to finding a site through public sector ownership is to acquire land or buildings that are currently in private ownership. Obviously all kinds of sites will be owned by all sorts of owners, and it may be quite idiosyncratic how groups will need to proceed with their liaisons and negotiations. There is, however, one key kind of private sector land-owner that groups could consider approaching, and that is the house-building sector itself. On the face of it this might seem a daft idea, approaching a house-building firm to enquire whether it has a site which it might be prepared to sell to another (community-based) developer. It is, however, the kind of transaction that the large house-building firms undertake all the time. A

large site is acquired, and formal permissions for use and development are obtained from the local planning authority. Next, 'parcels' of land are routinely offered to other house-building bodies – for cash, or on the basis of a site-by-site 'swop'. These developers build units on the site to complement what the main / first developer would wish to see, but with smaller-scale risk.

What this means for a cohousing group is that there is already a current practice to tap into where main developers are prepared to see other 'housing' bodies build on 'their' original site, if the nature of the proposed development is perceived as likely to add value to the main developer's overall site aspirations. In other words, the key task for the cohousing group is to be recognised as a credible body and that a cohousing neighbourhood taking shape on the wider site will add value to the total development. In fact, in the USA, as Stephen Hill has demonstrated, there are examples of private developers who have recognised that the consistent high quality of cohousing neighbourhoods does attract investors and purchasers to the wider development area. Some have even used pictures of cohousing properties within the developer's own promotional material!

When a cohousing group wishes to approach a main-stream house-building firm it does, of course, need to achieve 'credibility' in the minds of the firm. The group needs to demonstrate a logical business plan, alongside clear details of the kind of buildings and aesthetics it would construct, and about how all of this underlines what the cohousing facilities and characteristics would offer to the surrounding neighbourhoods.

And while a group could have a natural anxiety about how to negotiate the value of a site from a house-build-er, it can always: (a) check on the last price recorded for that site on the Land Registry website, with a follow up to the local authority's planning website to check on planning conditions associated with the site and any recent sale; (b) check the media (like *Estates Gazettes*) for contemporary examples of that site and any proposed development, (c) check local contacts in the development and house-building industry; (d) consider appointing an 'agent' to use their local skills and experience to negotiate a final sum and purchase conditions.

Finding sites via 'Neighbourhood Plans' or the 'Community Right to Build'

It is too early to know how the proposed new 'Community Right to Build' (CRTB) or the compilation of new 'Neighbourhood Plans' – as proposed in the Localism Bill – might in time identify sites suitable for the construction of 'community-led' developments, such as cohousing projects. Proposals for group-build schemes will certainly fit with what such new permissions are designed to encourage; however the requirement of the CRTB to win a majority support for the suggested use of a site as determined through a local referendum is very likely to bring concerns and conflicting ideas out into the open. A cohousing group that thinks a CRTB application could be the most appropriate means for its progress will need to can-vass the local community quite methodically, clearly explaining what cohousing is, and what it is not, in order that its proposals are clearly understood before putting such a 'right' formally in front of public opinion and the potential vagaries of local decision-making.

Details of organisations for finding sites or properties

1. Existing property

- *The Property Organisation* Unusual property for sale: castles, islands, houseboats, martello towers, churches, schools, windmills, watermills, pubs, barns
  www.property.org.uk/unique

- **www.pickupaproperty.com** - Property search service subscription

- **www.ruralscene.co.uk** - sell smallholdings, farms, residential holdings, properties with leisure facilities, woodland, water etc. in the UK and abroad.

2. Land plots

- Search formal 'Local Plan' of District, County, London Borough or Unitary Authority for land for identified residential development.

- Land Registry

- Plots of land for sale from UK Land Agents Directory **www.uklanddirectory.org.uk**

- **www.forestry.gov.uk/forestry/INFD-64NHHZ**

- *Estates Gazette*

3. Public sector and 'heritage' sites

- **www.homesandcommunities.co.uk/ourwork/land-and-development-opportunities**

- **www.mod.uk/DefenceEstates**

- **www.networkrail.co.uk/aspx/1590.aspx**

- **www.english-heritage.org.uk/caring/heritage-at-risk** – and **www.savebritainsheritage.org** – use of 'heritage' buildings at risk in England

- **www.buildingsatrisk.org.uk** – use of 'heritage' buildings at risk in Scotland

4. Agents acting across the UK

- **www.knightfrank.co.uk** - Estate agent specialising in sale of country houses, farms and estates and institutional properties.

- **www.struttandparker.co.uk** - Sale of farms and estates of all sizes

5. Potential 'free' land

Due to concern about the dubious nature of some offers of 'free land' that private adverts promote from time to time, The Land Registry has produced a guide 'Free land and property – advertisements about claiming land in England and Wales – The Land Registry Public Guide 16' available from their website. Land Registry's other guides provide guidance on other land use issues that can be problematic, such as 'Adverse possession of unregistered land and transitional provisions for registered land in the Land Registration Act 2002 – Land Registry Practice Guide 5'.

Towards the Future: Building 'Neighbourhoods in Trust'

MARTIN FIELD ET AL

Reflections by the Diggers & Dreamers editorial group and other contributors on the future of cohousing in Britain.

T he contributions in this publication detail the manner in which the sentiments and aspirations noted above have been informing progress within the UK's cohousing scene – its innovations, its international context and its feedback from 'cohousers' on living the vision in practice!

> *To form a cohousing community is to create an essentially local setting where neighbourliness is consciously sought after, with all that this means in terms of day to day casual interaction, mutual support and countless small acts of reciprocity between people who live in close proximity. The connecting theme of this book is that, in modern Western societies, this 'social capital' of neighbourliness has become harder to find and purposive action is therefore required to re-create it for the wellbeing of individuals and families and for the wider benefit of society, [... particularly] for older people, more tied to and dependent on locality ...*
> Maria Brenton

Cohousing is very, very clearly such a *purposive action* – carving out a local balance for households to thrive in 'closeness' *and* privacy, each finding their own level of ease with what they find has been deliberately placed on their doorsteps. And it works! In a host of different countries, and through many kinds of patronage, it delivers superb places in which people want to live, where children are safe to grow, and where 'caring' and 'sharing' are bywords for what has been built into the neighbourhood fabric. Even in the UK, where successful projects are only slowly coming into being, schemes are gaining awards, are being held up as 'exemplars' of sustainability, and are setting their mark for creating innovative and inclusive developments.

But it is not all unlimited success – all kinds of 'build' projects can come to grief and that has certainly been an outcome for some aspiring cohousing projects. Some groups have not achieved what they had hoped, even after years of hard efforts to find a site and bring in more members. And they disband when their frustration becomes unsupportable, and they see their vision being steadily suffocated. And if it has been difficult to carry some of these cohousing ambitions forward in the past, will there be aspects of the wider economic situation that impose even greater obstacles? It may be the intrinsic nature of 'free markets' that, besides their ups and downs, they contain a constantly changing set of *'opportunities'*. If so, the challenge to cohousing is to get to grips with what motivates policy-makers and opinion-formers, and to demonstrate its credibility for what it can offer to future plans for community and residential developments.

There is a major task to restore confidence in housing markets, change the current assessment of housing as a high risk investment, for both development finance and retail mortgages, and promote housing for its social and utility value rather than short-term speculation [....] an explicit aim of both the previous and current governments is to enable the emergence of a significant 'self-organised' and mixed-tenure housing sector that can unlock social, environmental and economic capital, at the least possible direct public cost [...] restoring confidence to the market to provide openings for complementary models of subsidised or affordable housing based on co-operative and mutual principles, either in joint ventures or standalone developments.

Stephen Hill

The UK's current political and economic climate represents one of those occasions when governmental concerns overlap with the concerns of economic markets and mainstream industry to stimulate viable business opportunities, along with local grassroots interests for what might happen in the future. In this case, these are all concerns about the fragile manner in which much recent housing and property investment has been undertaken, and the lack of 'sustainable' outcomes that seems to have been produced. At least for a while, there is a genuine readiness at senior levels to consider how local communities can be more centrally involved in shaping new developments, including an invigorated support for the mutual and communal route to local community development that intentional community groups have been quietly promoting over many years.

For over two decades Diggers & Dreamers has extolled the virtues of communal living. But this has largely been through the eyes of hard core communards who are prepared to share many facilities and live very closely with their fellow co-operators on a day-to-day basis. Sometimes this has been within big old houses in the country, sometimes within shared terraced buildings in cities. There has always been a realisation that this degree of communality is something of an acquired taste. The likelihood of a large proportion of the population suddenly – or even gradually – choosing to live in this way has always seemed very small indeed.

But the baby should never be thrown out with the bathwater. The cohousing model – with its considerable degree of privacy as well as access to many shared facilities – supplies a way of living in intentional community which would be very acceptable to many, many more people. At the same time – when compared with the average new build housing estate – it provides a huge step up in the base level of mutuality. With oil and other resources running out fast, the future for all of us is beginning to look very uncertain. It's clear that living within a supportive neighbourhood (where sharing is facilitated) could well turn an otherwise bleak existence into something quite pleasant. Cohousing communities will be streets ahead of everyone else on this and will have much to teach others.

So the sooner we have a larger number of examples in the UK the better. It is for this reason that Diggers & Dreamers is absolutely delighted at the current upsurge of interest in cohousing within this country and is very pleased to present this book of articles.
Jonathan How

Green Terrace – car free, converted terraced housing, illustration by Catriona Stamp.

1. Cycle store, built from recycled timber
2. Rain water catchment
3. Bat box and bird boxes
4. Upside – down living – kitchen/dining/living area upstairs, bedrooms downstairs
5. Grey-water collection
6. Solar water pre-heating

7 Commuter arriving home (via train and
   folding bike)
8 House with community facilities – office etc.
9 Wild-life-friendly garden, with pond, bird-
   feeders, shrubs for nectar and berries
10 Arbor cum climbing frame, with climbing plants
   seating area and just-for-fun windmill.
11 Community compost bins
12 Fruiting hedge

Supporters of cohousing projects will be keen to point out that while ideas come and go for how UK society could undertake a sustainable 'placemaking' (such is the nature of different fashions in urban design), cohousing remains a solid set of practical and demonstrable principles for creating attractive and treasured local spaces. Even when the cohousing focus is upon creating a sustainable scale for neighbourhoods, this need not be seen as a draw-back to making contributions to larger-scale built environments, for larger areas can be laid out on a 'modular' format[1] where cohousing neighbourhoods are juxtaposed with other neighbourhood areas that could be designed on other sets of criteria – for example, as a traffic-calmed 'Home Zone', or as a setting for other 'eco-housing' units.

The potential fit together of cohousing designs and other kinds of neighbourhood design can also highlight the scope for cohousing projects to be used to generate confidence in wider proposals for residential development. Private sector developers in the US are already wise to seeing that members of cohousing projects collectively amount to pre-contractual customers with a clear stake in the property and design standards the developer wishes to be seen to promote – they are even using publicity about the cohousing neighbourhoods sited within the wider developments to help 'suggest' the quality of the other residential development being proposed next door!

The inclusive and egalitarian values of cohousing's approach to 'community-led' initiatives is not tied to any particular tenure, nor reliant upon any one kind of finance: the UK's first schemes might have been led by 'private' funds but, as outlined in chapters above, its ability to establish mixed-tenure and mutually-owned projects can show how a group might now consider a variety of ways to secure 'inclusivity' and affordability:

Just as cohousing is defined to a large extent by conscious design and architecture, most schemes will remain unaffordable for many people until there is a financial architecture in place to allow rent, rent-to-buy, rent with equity or other schemes (like LILAC's pioneering model). Up until now, it has only been people who already own property who can join a cohousing scheme, but more diversity in financial systems will foster more diversity in the people who can participate in them.

Bunk

The 'self-organised' confidence and neighbourhood presence of UK cohousing projects has demonstrated sustained positive effects on local property valuations and a constant attraction to potential future residents, as well as demonstrating the ability to be accepted in time as an asset of the 'wider' local community, when social interactions organically and inevitably develop across adjoining neighbourhood and community boundaries.

While we find it very tempting to look towards chinks in official/government policy that cohousing could slip into and neatly match itself with rhetoric about sustainable communities and the 'Big Society', we are very wary of government involvement in intentional community building. There seems to be very little evidence of any useful past constructive involvement from government departments in self-help, bottom-up, community-led initiatives, and plenty that ought to ring alarm bells for anyone contemplating engaging with the devilish intricacies of government bureaucracy.

From the bastardisation of the Garden Village movement through to the brief courting of community self-build as flavour of the month/year by the Housing Corporation and Housing Associations in the 1980s, the 'helping hand' of government has so often proved in the end to be the kiss-of-death. Why should we think cohousing would be any different?

It may well be an oxymoron that governments (national, regional or local), by their very nature cannot deliver anything that is genuinely community-led and bottom-up. If they want to see residents take control of their own housing they need to remove the obstacles that they themselves have put in the way and have the good sense to step back and let people get on with it. Please, please, please let's not end up with an official policy on what cohousing should be, could be or is.

So if the way forward is not into the arms of the officialdom – which way for cohousing? We need to build on the experience of the 'pioneer' cohousing communities; we perhaps need a group of alternative developers and architects who have specialist skills at delivering cohousing (both the hardware and the software); we need local planning authorities to be more creative when thinking about community engagement and planning; we need financial institutions to look at putting enabling

*packages together so that each new group doesn't
need to renegotiate a deal with them; and perhaps
most of all we need to realise that we really do have
a tried and tested deliverable model of sustainable
community and just get on with it.*

Chris Coates

Advocates of the cohousing approach to neighbour-
hood-building will not be lost as to what they can
claim cohousing can deliver, given that there is much
that can be paraded as success from a modest number
of examples. If the incidence of such developments is
slow in the UK, it is unlikely to be because cohousing
is struggling to justify the benefits of planning and
creating new homes in the collective context of the
places in and around them, but more that this is still
quite distinct from the predominant ethos of how most
residential areas are being speculatively built and
populated. Cohousing can in fact adopt a stance from
the Community Land Trust movement to highlight what
it always intends to create: '*neighbourhoods in trust,
homes that last*'. It would be a fitting benchmark to
carry forward as a challenge to those aspiring to high
quality 'place-making' in the future.

Note
1   See presentation to Northampton Institute for
    Urban Affairs on 'Integrated Sustainable Design
    Solutions for Modular Neighbourhoods', (2010)

My boy was born today, where will he play?
Will he play indoors on his own, all alone?
Will he play in the road, with the cars?
Will he play in the park, far away?
Let us get rid of the cars.
Let us know our neighbours.
Let us build a community together.
Let us talk in the streets, with no cars.
Let the children play.
Let the adults play.
Let the old people play.
Let the children play.

Richard Delorenzi,
Community Land Trusts conference, 2010

Appendices

Appendix A
A Resumé of Characteristics of Cohousing Neighbourhoods

MARTIN FIELD

Further detail on the essential characteristics of cohousing neighbourhoods[1] :

(a) Designing for 'intentional neighbourhoods'

Cohousing communities have been developed within discrete neighbourhoods whose layout makes deliberate use of architectural and design features to maximise intentional and incidental social contact between neighbours. A familiar example of this is that private internal rooms where people spend a significant amount of time (like kitchen areas) are placed to look out towards external communal spaces where neighbours are walking or relaxing, in order to generate spontaneous opportunities for residents to make visual or verbal contact together.

Cohousing neighbourhoods are moreover invariably vehicle-free, with the use of any cars restricted to parking or garage areas at the edge of the neighbourhood area, in order to maximise other space for pedestrian and leisure use. There may be some small individual garden areas for household use, but these are generally modest in size in order to encourage neighbours to meet and mix together in the neighbourhood's wider open and recreational spaces.

(b) The minimum provision of private and common facilities

All households in cohousing neighbourhoods have private and self-contained accommodation – ie they all have sole private use of their own domestic living, eating, cooking and washing spaces. This is, however, usually supplemented by other facilities within the wider neighbourhood that are shared and used by all the community's households. Such shared facilities could include a laundry, guest accommodation, and rooms for craft and hobby activities – some cohousing settings have barns, greenhouses, garages, workshops, and a sports ground!

The design and location of a common building or common house is crucial, since it will be a venue for communal facilities, as well as the place where community members come together, particularly to share meals. While there is no standard blueprint for such 'common facilities', a minimum would be that they allow for the preparation and enjoyment of sharing meals and be of a sufficient size for all the households and community members to meet together for joint activities, whenever this is desired.

(c) Community size and scale to support community dynamics

Cohousing communities have recognised that there is an important balance to achieve between creating a common sense of identity in a neighbourhood, and sustaining a sufficient level of privacy for each household. In practice, this means that cohousing communities recognise that the scale of their settings has to pay attention to both personal and interpersonal dimensions – to how big or how small it is. There is a recognition that the sense of being part of a 'community' nevertheless needs to accommodate times when some households may choose or need to be private and not feel obliged to participate in communal activities, without their absence constraining other communal activities or dynamics.

There is also the recognition that the total size of the neighbourhood population should enable all members to know one another and be known on a personal basis, and not be so large a group that such familiarity is too difficult to sustain. If cohousing has one key 'sustainable dynamic' it is arguably this attention given to the scale of neighbourhood development. It should not be so small as to be over-powering in pressing households to interact constantly together, but neither too big as to be beyond sustaining meaningful contact and relationships with the other households in that neighbourhood. While individual households will obviously vary in their separate make-up of ages and sizes, a rule-of-thumb from Danish commentators for a viable size of the wider community is that the number of adults will be somewhere between about ten and forty.

(d) Residents' control and management of their own neighbourhoods

The residents of a cohousing neighbourhood are always responsible for all the aspects of its creation and operation. This invariably starts in the managing of formalities for the planning, design and financing arrangements required at each stage of the neighbourhood's development, and often includes making and then managing professional appointments to carry out the different construction, legal and technical necessities of such development.

The residents will also be collectively responsible for managing the neighbourhood and its facilities. Any difference between the individual tenure of households will not matter here – all the households will collectively agree to 'rules' of the neighbourhood, have a say in choosing new member-households in the future, and share and agree the ongoing costs of the neighbourhood and communal facilities and any other service charges.

Note

1. An abridgement of text taken from 'Thinking about Cohousing', Diggers & Dreamers Publications, 2004.

Appendix B
Some Distinctions Between Cohousing and Community Land

MARTIN FIELD

Given the above restatement of cohousing's core characteristics, it would perhaps be a little pedantic to repeat verbatim how cohousing has been distinguished in the past from other kinds of neighbourhood or community housing provision. What is more appropriate is to take a moment to reflect on how cohousing may compare with the attention given to the growing popularity of Community Land Trusts (CLTs), as a focus for providing new and affordable housing for local people.

The growing interest in the development of Community Land Trusts in the UK already attests to how they might address local community and housing needs. Some

CLTs are principally focused on achieving a local and shared land-use, such as for food production, rather than on built development for housing purposes; what follows looks principally at housing-centred CLTs. In a spirit that is certainly akin to the promotion of cohousing projects, CLTs want to establish sustainable local housing in which local people will have a clear lead. The design of CLTs could even incorporate the essential characteristics of cohousing neighbourhoods, if its promoters were so minded, and a sensitive suggestion of the facilities of a cohousing-shaped CLT being available to other local people in its vicinity might strengthen a CLT's potential to gain support from a host community! In the main, however, plans for CLT provision in the UK have been small in scale – certainly smaller in scale and site size than what Appendix A states as a fundamental minimum for cohousing projects. This would suggest they would be below the size for a recognisably cohousing 'dynamic' to emerge.

The range in the motivating and decision-making factors behind CLT schemes is also extremely broad, to the extent whereby an acceptable 'accountability' to local people does not require the resident-managed approach of cohousing areas. At one end of this spectrum of projects are CLT bodies whose ambitions are largely steered by the households looking to be housed in CLT property. At the other end, however, CLT bodies are demonstrating a more 'philanthropic' attitude, whereby local members of a community wish to secure new resources in order to build local affordable housing for local households in need – but to be organised through a Management Board structure that is comprised of local supporters, rather than from the households themselves. (Securing charitable status for the CLT body may indicate that it will not be open to ultimate control by resident households themselves.) To date, the main CLT provision in the UK has principally been of the 'philanthropic' kind. Their focus has been very firmly on securing the means to provide affordable housing for local households (both to rent and for low-cost ownership). A strong motivating factor for CLT developments has been to provide new housing that can fit with the fabric of each host community, rather than a specific approach to developing any wider intentionally-minded neighbourhood. This has also meant that such CLT projects have not sought to provide other kinds of shared neighbourhood facilities that would go into a recognisable cohousing area, along with the residential dwellings.

What is however very telling about the growing momentum of the UK's CLT movement is the relative acceptance of the concept of 'land trusts' by both local decision-takers and wider policy-makers, and the degree of success this is already producing for schemes on the ground. CLT's overt promotion of local affordable housing is likely to be a crucial factor in gaining local support, as the provision of such housing is at the front of many current local priorities, before that of creating whole new neighbourhoods. This contrasts fairly starkly with the reception experienced by many cohousing proposals during the past few years, where, despite the commitment and hard endeavours of groups looking to secure cohousing-focused resources, a similar degree of local support and success has simply not been achieved. Is this because local supporters of CLT schemes are more likely to have direct access to local land, than cohousing's proponents? Or is it because local CLT ambitions can proceed on smaller sites than would be feasible for cohousing development? It should no longer be the case that cohousing is seen as only providing for more affluent households, rather than those in need (as sought by CLTs).The examples of the Threshold and LILAC schemes clearly demonstrate that cohousing is now making real advances in the range of tenures it can provide in the UK: there are certainly no longer grounds for seeing such developments as incompatible with equivalent-sized CLT proposals.

Appendix C
The UK Cohousing Network

MARTIN FIELD

The UK Cohousing Network was formed following the Lancaster Cohousing Conference in February 2005 and has become the key body providing information and advice on cohousing schemes in the UK.

The Network is a Company Limited by Guarantee (No 6313462), with a registered address at the Community project in Lewes (15 Laughton Lodge, Laughton, Lewes, East Sussex, BN8 6BY). It operates via a Board that is comprised of people from established and forming cohousing groups, giving their time voluntarily.

The aims of the Network are to:

- Develop as a resource point for individuals and forming-cohousing groups

- Develop and maintain the cohousing website

- Promote and signpost conferences, seminars and workshops on cohousing issues

- Raise awareness of cohousing and promote this via the media

- Undertake lobbying and policy development with government contacts

- Provide an advice point for formal bodies and professionals in the planning, housing, development and community design sectors

- Seek ways of making cohousing as financially accessible as possible.

In its initial stages, the Network secured a small grant from the Co-operative Fund to help it become established, and it looks regularly at making applications to other grant-making bodies to secure funds that can help cover its modest overheads. For example, it has been able to secure funds from the 'Age Unlimited' programme developed by National Endowment for Science, Technology and the Arts (NESTA) to help promote and develop opportunities for Older People'sCohousing projects. This project is typical of the area of work with which the Network is keen to engage – policy development, combined with practical advice for how particular projects could get off the ground. As already mentioned, the Network was a part of the Commission for Mutual and Co-operative Housing, and members have continued to contribute to the development of the Mutual Housing Sector Group (chaired by Nic Bliss, who edited the Commission's report) in order to have a clear and consistent national advocacy of all kinds of community-led housing and neighbourhood initiatives.

The basic members of the UK Network are UK cohousing groups and projects. Its current modest size means it is not able to generate levels of membership contributions for it to operate on a par with larger organisations that have full-time personnel. The Network Board is therefore looking at how it can develop to meet the needs of different interests in cohousing; how it might regularise contact with groups and established communities; and at the finances to help it and cohousing become more sustainable.

The website address of the UK Cohousing Network is:

www.cohousing.org.uk

Users who access the Network's web-pages will be able to find the following kinds of information:

- A mix of general articles and explanations about cohousing for individuals interested in cohousing and for professional and media contacts.

- A map of the UK with icons giving the location of all current groups and projects.

- A description of various completed (established) cohousing communities.

- A list of developing groups and the stages of their individual work.

- A series of links to various resources in the UK and abroad: web-links; books, DVDs and other publications; case studies; and courses.

- A series of archives that give media articles and references, and a summary of information and news presented over time by the UK Network.

New items of information flag themselves up when the website is immediately accessed – such as a new document that summarises frequently-asked questions and answers about cohousing and scheme development.

The website also provides a form of bill-board to advertise cohousing property that could be up for sale in different locations, and on other cohousing-related investment opportunities (for example, LILAC has used this facility to promote the possibility of investment in co-op loan stock).

Finally there is a 'contact us' facility that allows users to send in a request for information or submit comments. At times this is combined with a survey to collect views on an aspect of the Network's engagements.

[Note: like all websites there is a constant process of development and refinement in order to try and keep its format and content as topical and applicable to as many users as possible – the Network welcomes feedback on what the website could contain and how to maximise its benefit to cohousing groups.]

Appendix D
Ideas for Researching Cohousing Issues in the UK

CHRISTINA CERULLI AND MARTIN FIELD

Communal, mutual and collaborative models of residential development are increasingly emerging as powerful propositions to address the changing social, environmental and economic contexts in which they are taking place. In both 'user-produced' and academic literature there is evidence of a renewed, growing interest in communal housing solutions and in shared and collaboratively developed facilities for recreation and living, alongside a corresponding interest in any increased participation in neighbouring and community activities.

One of the key underlying themes in academic and non-academic literature is the link between communal forms of living and wellbeing with particular reference to the implicit encouragement of neighbouring activities, social interaction and the strengthening of a 'sense of community'. Research into neighbourhoods, social interaction and wellbeing highlights the need for studies looking at neighbourhood and community boundaries as they are used and experienced, rather than as defined by census data. Communal housing is in many ways a 'special case', as social interaction and the rethinking of community boundaries are often central to both their development and day-to-day running. By studying the ways in which social interactions develop within different types of communal housing and in their surrounding neighbourhoods, research should help develop a wider understanding of what is distinct in communal housing schemes from their wider socio-economic context.

Research and academic networks such as the 'International Association of People-Environment Studies', the 'Intentional Communal Studies Association' and the 'Utopian Studies Society' have been exploring the interrelation of people and the environment for years. Other networks of like-minded community endeavours, such as the 'Fellowship for Intentional Communities' and the 'Global Ecovillage Network', have devoted close examination to how sustainable communal housing models offer the potential to reduce building footprints, energy use and living costs. Books and articles that systematically expand on the potential for a more egalitarian and equitable society routinely examine how communal housing typically questions the conventional division of public and private space, and the notion of caring, both for others and for the environment. Indeed, this is often cited as one of the main drivers behind collaborative and co-operative schemes.

However, despite this extensive work there is still something of a lack in the literature of systematic study into the exemplars of communal housing projects, and their wider spatial and architectural significance in a given historic context. Research into the areas of wellbeing, social interaction and the built environment to date has tended to remain discipline-specific: psychology has tended to focus on the sense of community and use patterns of 'neighbourhoods', while public health and urban planning often approach 'wellbeing' through comparing attitudes of relocated residents. Few texts make explicit reference to the actual design of intentional communal housing developments or attempt to make salient connections to them. There is a need for cross-disciplinary research on the actual design of communal housing and neighbourhood schemes and for wider discussion around the socio-economic impact of developing and living in such settings.

In order to gauge the limits and opportunities for cohousing development in the UK today, and to explore what type, model and focus of research might offer support here, it will help to situate cohousing within the wider context of communal housing and neighbourhoods research, whilst also looking at pulling together information on the kinds of research currently taking place and examining what drivers have brought that forward.

A few themes for potential research into UK Cohousing settings are noted below.

Holistic understanding of precedents

Whilst there is no shortage of histories and accounts of some types of communal housing, there is relatively little on what has ante-dated cohousing as a communal form, nor on what other housing or neighbourhood forms had been influenced by any such precedents, at the time when they were being promoted. For research to inform contemporary practice and design there is a need to study the impact of cohousing-type models at individual and community level in their historic context, and to examine any social and wellbeing implications for current trends and opportunities on communal and collaborative projects.

Design and spatial arrangement

Notwithstanding the substantial literature that exists on how to design cohousing communities, much less research has been published that has given a critical look at the 'hardware' as well as the 'software' of cohousing developments – communal places need to be analysed in terms of their spatial arrangement and balance of public, private and mediating spaces, and compared against what has been 'asked' of them. Feedback is required from cohousing residents as the mediators, evaluating how their localities perform in practice, how buildings are used and interpreted over time, and if they satisfy their respective original design intentions.

Costs and resources

There is a prevalent belief that cohousing must be a fairly expensive form of built development, at least in the UK, given that such settings appear to include more facilities than conventional or new housing estate layouts. Hard data is required to support or challenge that view, and to provide a more transparent set of insights into the different kinds of operational costs and benefits once schemes have been created.

Perceptions from 'communal users'

There is an opportunity to conceptualise research around cohousing in UK in a way that aligns with the ethos of it being a lived-in example of 'collective production'. User (resident) perceptions will include all kinds of related experiences and views on the project's procurements and what has constituted 'success', as well as on its conflicts, crises and 'failures'. Research then becomes a review of a collaborative effort where multiple voices and perspectives are invited and where prior conventions in terms of authority, legitimacy and professional recognition may be challenged.

Christina Cerulli
works at the University of Sheffield's Department of Architecture

Appendix E
Books and Websites

CHRIS COATES AND
MARTIN FIELD

Further resources
The following is a select list/contact details of recent publications and other reports related to cohousing:

- FIELD, Martin. *Thinking About CoHousing: the creation of intentional neighbourhoods.* Diggers & Dreamers Publications, (2004),
  ISBN: 0-9514945-7-0
  [Diggers & Dreamers original publication on cohousing in the UK, still providing a useful presentation of what groups should consider to gain support for local schemes.]

- VESTBRO, Dick Urban (ed). *Living Together – Cohousing Ideas & Realities Around the World.* Proceedings of International Collaborative Housing Conference, Sweden, (2010), ISBN: 978-91-7415-738-3
  [A variety of pieces that convey the breadth of approach taken at this auspicious conference, including the main speakers and short summaries of the different workshops.]

- MELTZER,Graham. *Sustainable Community: learning from the cohousing model.* Trafford, (2005) ISBN: 1-4120-4994-6
  [Material compiled for a PhD award, containing some useful overviews of cohousing schemes established in the US.]

- *Affordable Cohousing : turning vision into reality*

[Background note to event on 24 May 2010 hosted by Hanover and supported by the UK Cohousing Network, the National Housing Federation and Age UK, Hanover Housing (2010).]

- *Draft National Planning Policy Framework*, Department of Communities & Local Government, HMSO, (2011), ISBN: 978-1-4098-3048-1 [The Coalition Government's framework to encourage greater community participation in UK planning issues, while also helping to stimulate more house building and supply.]

- *An Action Plan to Promote the Growth of Self Build Housing*, The Report of the Self Build Government-Industry Working Group, National Self Build Association, 2011 [An Action Plan and set of proposals for how to stimulate community-led house-building, including of cohousing schemes, with detail of UK cohousing projects as examples.]

- *Community Right to Build*, **www.communities.gov.uk/righttobuild** (2011) [Detail of the Coalition Government's referendum-led process for local community-backed schemes to secure a practical 'right' to build new projects on identified sites.]

- *Homes and Community Agency website (2011) on land disposals*: **www.homesandcommunities.co.uk/ourwork/ land-and-development-opportunities** [New web-based information on how the Agency is intending to dispose / sell public land and assets.]

- *The Land & Society Commission Report*, Royal Institution of Chartered Surveyors, (2011) [An independent report from a Committee established by the RICS to examine 'how all parts of the property industry can support communities' in the context of the Coalition Government's plans for 'localism' – contains very useful recommendations.]

- *Who should build our homes?*, archived publication from CABE – Commission on

Architecture and the Built Environment
**http://webarchive.nationalarchives.gov.uk/
2011011 8095356
http://www.cabe.org.uk/publications/
listing?tag=Housing&tagId=22&type=publications**
[A variety of perspectives on what interests
or formal bodies should be encouraged to be
engaged with future house-building, including a
couple of visions for community-led approaches
like cohousing and other Land Trusts.]

- BLISS, Nic (ed). *Bringing Democracy Home*,
  Commission on Co-operative and Mutual
  Housing, (2009), ISBN: 978-0-9564332-0-6
  [A milestone in the recent attention given to
  modern examples of 'mutual' housing provision,
  with significant mention of cohousing projects,
  and the background to the formation of the
  Mutual Housing Sector group that includes
  representation from the UK Cohousing Network.]

- *Anchors of Tomorrow : a vision for community
  organisations of the future*, Community
  Alliance, (2009)
  [A key summary document from the 'community
  development sector' of how community-owned
  assets can be a cornerstone of sustainable
  neighbourhood development.]

- LAMBERT, Blaise (ed). *Financing Co-operative
  and Mutual Housing*, Confederation of
  Co-operative Housing, (2010)
  www.cch.coop/bcmh/docs
  [A form of 'manifesto' from the Mutual Housing
  sector looking to identify key housing bodies
  and local authorities willing to become engaged
  in plans for new 'mutual' housing schemes,
  utilising a framework for significant funding
  from the private finance sector.]

- *What is Mutual Home Ownership?*,
  **www.cds.coop/about-us/
  mutual-home-ownership**
  [Detail on this relatively new form of collective
  ownership in the UK, as being used by LILAC in
  Leeds.]

- *Community-led Procedure Guide*. Homes and
  Community Agency (2011)
  www.homesandcommunities.co.uk

[A new procedure (to be publicly available from Autumn 2011) on how 'community-led' housing projects could apply for some grant funding towards some of their project's build costs, if it meets the criteria for this procedure and for the use of grant from the Coalition Government's new 'Affordable Housing' programme.]

• • • • • • • • • • • • • • • • • • • •

Lancaster Cohousing found the following books useful. They are available from the following websites:
www.cohousing.org/mkt/bookstore
http://store.ic.org/catalog/
www.amazon.co.uk

- SCOTT HANSON, Kelly & Chris. *The Cohousing Handbook; Building a Place for Community.* New Society Publishers (2004)

- LEACH, Shari. *Head, Heart and Hands: Lessons in Community Building* (2005), Wonderland Hill Development Company

- LEAFE CHRISTIAN, Diana. *Creating a Life Together: Practical Tools to Grow Ecovillages and Intentional Communities.* New Society Publishers (2002)

- McCAMANTm Kathryn & DURRETT, Charles. *Cohousing : A Contemporary Approach to Housing Ourselves* (2010)

- DURRETT, Chuck. *Senior Cohousing : A Community Approach to Independent Living* (2010)

- *Building United Judgment: A Handbook for Consensus Decision-making,* edited by Center for Conflict Resolution, re-published by the Fellowship for Intentional Community, ISBN: 0-9602714-6-5

- BROWN, Juanita & ISAACS, David. *The World Café: Shaping Our Futures Through Conversations that Matter* (2010) ISBN-10: 1576752585

Also useful help/info/training from:
www.seedsforchange.org.uk

Isn't it time you explored the Edge of Time solar system?

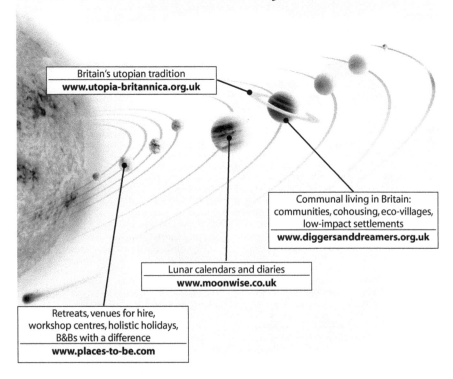

Britain's utopian tradition
www.utopia-britannica.org.uk

Communal living in Britain:
communities, cohousing, eco-villages,
low-impact settlements
www.diggersanddreamers.org.uk

Lunar calendars and diaries
www.moonwise.co.uk

Retreats, venues for hire,
workshop centres, holistic holidays,
B&Bs with a difference
www.places-to-be.com

Edge of Time Ltd
BCM Edge
London
WC1N 3XX
Telephone 020 8133 1451
E-mail sales@edgeoftime.co.uk

www.edgeoftime.co.uk

Lightning Source UK Ltd.
Milton Keynes UK
UKHW010014270620
365635UK00001B/53